Recollections of a Romanian Diplomat 1918–1969

VOLUME TWO

Recollections of a Romanian Diplomat 1918–1969

Diaries and Memoirs of Raoul V. Bossy

VOLUME TWO

EDITED AND TRANSLATED BY
G. H. and M.-A. Bossy

HOOVER INSTITUTION PRESS
STANFORD UNIVERSITY   STANFORD, CALIFORNIA

The Hoover Institution on War, Revolution and Peace, founded at Stanford University in 1919 by Herbert Hoover, who went on to become the thirty-first president of the United States, is an interdisciplinary research center for advanced study on domestic and international affairs. The views expressed in its publications are entirely those of the authors and do not necessarily reflect the views of the staff, officers, or Board of Overseers of the Hoover Institution.

www.hoover.org

Hoover Institution Press Publication No. 507

First printing, 2003
09 08 07 06 05 04 03 9 8 7 6 5 4 3 2 1

Manufactured in the United States of America

Cover and frontispiece photo by Ernst Schnaider, Berlin.
Book design by Kelly J. Applegate, Publication Services.

The paper used in this publication meets the minimum requirements of the American National Standard for Information Sciences—Permanence of Paper for Printed Library Materials, ANSI Z39.48–1984.

Library of Congress Cataloging-in-Publication Data

Bossy, Raoul V., 1894–1975
[Souvenirs d'un diplomate. English]
Recollections of a Romanian diplomat, 1918–1969: diaries and memoirs of Raoul V. Bossy / edited and translated by G. H. and M.-A. Bossy.
p.cm. — (Archival documentary)
Includes bibliographical references and index.
ISBN 0-8179-2951-7 (alk. paper)
1. Romania—Foreign relations—1914–1944. 2. Bossy, Raoul V., 1894–1975–Diaries. 3. Diplomats—Romania—Diaries. I. Bossy, George H. II. Bossy, Michel-André, III. Bossy, Raoul V., 1894–1975. Memoirs of a diplomat. IV. Title. V. Series.

DR264 .B67413 2002
327.498092—dc21
[B]

2002017255

Contents

Volume Two

10

Rome (1939–1940)

I. 1939

I arrived in Bucharest on October 5, in order to see the king and the government before joining my new post.

My first official visit was, obviously, to the foreign minister, my old childhood friend Grigore Gafencu. He told me that Ciano had requested the recall of my predecessor, Alexandru Duiliu Zamfirescu, who was no longer persona grata at the Palazzo Chigi "because he caroused too much and because he stepped beyond the pale on policy matters." Zamfirescu had boasted that the king had entrusted him with a special mission to Mussolini, intended to bring about a tangible rapprochement between Italy and Romania, and he had of course been disavowed. It was therefore necessary that I should leave for Rome as soon as possible, so that the new Romanian envoy might wash out the bad taste left by the preceding one.

Turning to the political side of my mission, Gafencu told me that our leaders would welcome the creation of a neutral bloc of nations in Southeastern Europe. Under the aegis of Italy, such a bloc would try to keep the war from spreading to one of the continent's most volatile zones and sensitive nerve centers. All the same, I was cautioned in succession by Carol II, Prime Minister Argetoianu, and Foreign Minister Gafencu to let the Italian government make the first move. In other words: wait and see. The creation of such a bloc of states could raise concerns among both the Allies and the Russians, the Allies being uneasy about the leading role that would be assumed by Italy, and the Russians being always very touchy when it came to the Balkans. In any event, according to Gafencu, this neutral Balkan bloc would have to include Turkey (which happened to have just signed a treaty with France and Britain), for the sake of balance. For his part, however, the foreign minister preferred to clarify our relations with Russia before setting out on such a path. And he urged me, in the meantime, to keep an eye on the little "barbs" that the Italians kept thrusting, so it seemed, against their German partners.

There followed a long series of official visits. An extended visit with Prime Minister Argetoianu, a courtesy call on Bárdossy ("You were loved in Budapest, the princess[1] and you"), a first official contact with Pellegrino Ghigi, Italy's envoy to Bucharest, an audience with the king, calls on various members of the government, and two more visits with Gafencu. I also met with Pamfil Şeicaru,[2] who was pessimistic about the domestic political outlook. The executions following Călinescu's assassination could prove disastrous for us, since "it is impermissible for a state to take revenge." Ghigi also gave a luncheon in my honor, where I met all his collaborators, who made tactless and disagreeable allusions to poor Zamfirescu, imagining no doubt that they were pleasing me. What lack of taste, and even of manners! I was especially delighted to find among the guests dear Alexander Lahovary, who had twice been my boss in Rome.

I left Bucharest on October 17, arriving the next day in Venice, where I was met by my predecessor. As usual, I checked in at the Danieli. Poor Zamfirescu, too, told me the causes of his abrupt recall. Prodded on by Guaranta di Zullino (Magdalena Lahovary's husband), he tried to feel out the Italian government on the possibility of a secret understanding between Italy and Romania. When Guaranta informed him that Mussolini was ready to receive him to hear "the king's proposal," Zamfirescu had to beat a retreat, since Bucharest "didn't want to go along." Furious, Ciano instructed Ghigi to tell Gafencu that Zamfirescu was no longer persona grata in Rome.

FIRST CONTACTS

On October 20 my train pulled into Rome, which I had left twelve years earlier with the rank of first secretary. As custom bids, I had tossed two *soldi* over my shoulder into the Trevi Fountain for good fortune to return to Rome, and the fountain had kept faith with me. I was greeted at the station by an aide from Palazzo Chigi and by the staffs of our

[1]Mrs. Senta Bossy, née Princess Cantacuzino.
[2]Leading Romanian journalist.

two legations, one for the Quirinal and one for the Vatican. That evening I dined with a few of my new staff at the grill of the Albergo degli Ambasciatori. No sooner were we seated at our table than Ciano made his entrance, surrounded by a large and merry retinue. Passing close to us he recognized me, since we had seen each other several times in Budapest. He shook hands and welcomed me "unofficially, in anticipation of the official greeting a few days from now."

The following day I paid my obligatory visit to the chief of protocol, the *capo cerimoniale,* who was an old acquaintance, Andrea Geisser Celesia di Vegliasco. He let me know that a great sorrow was troubling his boss: Ciano's sister, Countess Maria Magistrati, wife of the Italian embassy counselor in Berlin, was on her deathbed. I would therefore have to wait a few days before being officially greeted by the foreign minister.

Within only three days, however, Ciano summoned me to the Palazzo Chigi. I crossed again, after a twelve-year interval, its marvelous chambers with their splendid ceilings and handsome Flemish tapestries, until I entered the great stateroom in which Mussolini's son-in-law held official court. The meeting began on a sad note, since I had to offer him my condolences and those of Gafencu for the loss of his sister, of whom he was so fond. Ciano was deeply moved and his eyes watered. He no longer looked like a big-time Fascist throwing out his chest, thrusting his jaw, and bellowing his words. He was a man grieving out of heartfelt family attachment. "She was only thirty-three," he said, "a flower has been ripped out." He pulled himself together. He asked me to convey his thanks to Gafencu, adding amiably that he also thanked him for naming an envoy in Rome with whom he had exchanged such interesting conversations in Budapest.

Moving on, he questioned me right away about our relations with the Hungarians—for, he went on to observe, "our relations with your country are merely 'correct,' whereas with Greece they are good [*sic*], with Yugoslavia very good, and with Hungary excellent—and that is directly on account of the frictions that exist between Bucharest and Budapest." I replied that tensions between us and our neighbors to the west were easing now, to say the least: Regent Horthy and his foreign minister, Count Csáky, had both been pleased to state as much during their last meetings with me. Csáky had even declared to me, "What draws us together even more than our negotiations are our common dangers." Dangers from the east and also from the west, since neither of our nations wished to submit to a Communist or Nazi regime.

Ciano took note of what I had just told him, and he stressed how it confirmed what he had heard from other sources. The road was therefore open toward a new Italian-Romanian friendship, which would aptly overlay the old bonds between two Latin sister nations. Nevertheless, he was worried by the pact sealed in Ankara between Britain, Turkey, and France, which in its third article reaffirmed the well-known Franco-British security pledge, which Romania similarly enjoyed. I replied that the pledge to which he alluded would in no way pull the Balkan Entente away from the neutral moorings it had chosen for itself. Indeed, that guarantee would, more likely than not, build peace in that part of Europe, were it matched by a similar pledge on the part of the Axis powers. Ciano had already pictured us all driven by Paris and London into a conflict that would overwhelm our capacities to resist and survive. "And yet," he declared with a sudden hint of buoyancy, "neutrality would clearly be the wisest course of action for the Balkan Entente: of what help is the Franco-British pledge? Its inadequacy has been shown well enough in the case of Poland. Now, if you were to obtain Germany's pledge or that of Russia, it would be a different matter, of course! That would be of some value, for it would be based on geographical realities. I tried to explain this to Gafencu, but he didn't heed my advice. It was a mistake, and he also blundered when he spoke to the Duce about French-Italian relations instead of confining his remarks to Romania. The Duce doesn't like the Titulescu fashion, that habit of meddling in major European affairs."

I dared interrupt this intricate tirade: "Unfortunately, the interests of my country are so closely tied to those of major powers and its fate is so dependent on good relations among the 'great powers' that a Romanian statesman has both the right and the obligation to do everything he can in order to further the reconciliation of Europe's divergent interests. For that reason, the 'European' diplomacy practiced by Titulescu was first and foremost a Romanian diplomacy. The same is true of the present foreign minister. When he seeks to encourage a Franco-Italian rapprochement, his sole aim, in the final analysis, is to preserve his own country from being flung in spite of itself into a new conflagration."

"I don't deny his good intentions," Ciano retorted, "and I like Gafencu, but I persist in saying that small or middle-sized countries should not intervene in the quarrels among major powers, and that, moreover, it would be in their best interest to make geographical factors a central consideration of their foreign policy. Austria, Czechoslovakia, and Poland have perished because they failed to do so. In Poland's case, another unfortunate component must be mentioned: Beck's neurotic vanity. When you are a midget, you remain short even if you climb on a table. Beck deluded himself into thinking that by proclaiming daily at the top of his voice that Poland was a major power it would indeed become one. But getting back to the tripartite Ankara pact, Italy dislikes it because it grants Turkey an exaggerated ascendancy in the Balkans. And let's not forget that Italy is itself a major Balkan power, now that it stretches over Albania!" I could not refrain a secret smile, imagining Ciano getting onto a table like Beck in order to proclaim at the top of his voice that by holding the Albanian coastline Italy had become a great Balkan power. People always see the mote in their neighbor's eye, and never the beam in their own!

Our conversation slid onto projects for a neutral Balkan bloc. Ciano alleged that such projects left him cold. Did he mean it? He did cautiously add, "for the time being"; and he further said that there would be no harm in putting out feelers and exchanging views. The real war had not yet started, he observed, thanks to Italy's very firm stance. "Although we are allied to Germany, we have not been asked to take part. You saw that during the exchange of telegrams between Hitler and Mussolini. Besides, why would we have become involved in a war that did not concern us in any way? We are not neutral, we are nonbelligerent, and for that reason we want to maintain good relations with everyone, so as to be able to preserve peace in Southeastern Europe."

As the meeting drew to an end, Ciano informed me that I would be asked to present my credentials to Victor Emmanuel III early in November, when his majesty would leave San Rossore and return to his winter quarters at the Villa Savoia. The Duce, for his part, ever since the beginning of the war, no longer officially greeted the heads of foreign missions, from lack of time (or courtesy?), but when the first opportunity arose he would enable me to contact him "in private fashion." Showing me out, Ciano took me by the arm and urged us to rent the Villa Ruspoli on the Janiculum as seat of the Romanian legation. The villa belonged to Eugenio and Dora Ruspoli, great friends of his, and he told me that he loved to spend evenings there, looking at the lights of Rome and listening to the murmur of the Paola Fountain. I consented, provided my government agreed, but I stipulated a condition: when I was the tenant of that dream house, he should continue his frequent visits to contemplate the majestic views. Chuckling, he promised to do so, and as we shook hands on the threshold, he gestured grandly toward the beautiful room and said, "This room is yours, come whenever you please." I did not take this invitation fully at face value, yet I told myself that once in a while I might discreetly avail myself of what he was authorizing, and I thanked him for this cordial first encounter. It was, after all, a rather auspicious beginning for the tough assignment that lay ahead.

The following day, in a report to my government, I commented on Ciano's declarations to me, and I stated my impression that the tripartite Ankara pact had profoundly upset the Fascist leadership, in spite of reassurances proffered by the British and French ambassadors. Under the noncommittal utterances of the press one fathomed bitterness.

In his lead article for the *Giornale d'Italia,* the celebrated Virginio Gayda, Ciano's spokesman, used the same language as his boss did with me to underscore that Italy not only counted in the Balkans but was a major power, controlling longer borders in Albania than Turkey held in western Thrace. The break-off of negotiations between Saracioglu and Molotov had been highly pleasing to Palazzo Chigi, where, in spite of repeated claims of loyalty to Germany, Italy was busily subverting the friendly understanding between Berlin and Moscow, for ideological reasons and also because such an entente of course pushed Italy backstage in Hitler's international political system. At the same time, Mussolini hoped that nothing else would ensue after the collapse of Russian-Turkish negotiations and that he would be able to pursue diplomatic activities in the Balkans with an entirely free hand.

Now, however, the Allies had succeeded in uniting London, Paris, and Ankara: that development served to strengthen the Balkan Entente and was likely to foul up Mussolini's game plan, in which he already pictured himself at the head of a neutral Balkan bloc. Moreover, the Ankara pact envisioned a possible future aggression by Italy in the Mediterranean, and that came across as an unfriendly gesture. I therefore believed that we could expect Fascist diplomacy to make persistent efforts to sow division among the countries of the Balkan Entente. This, among other reasons, helped to explain the rapprochement between Rome, Budapest, and Belgrade, and Italy's backing of Magyar grievances was a means of pressuring Bucharest.

✧ ✧ ✧

On the morning of November 18, Marquess Marini-Clarelli, master of ceremonies at court, came to fetch me at the Villa Ruspoli, in a splendid carriage with a coachman and three footmen in red and gold full livery plus powdered wigs, all in order to drive me to the Quirinal so that I could present my credentials to King Victor Emmanuel III. We were all in full-dress uniforms. Several other carriages pulled up to convey the staff of my legation. The long procession that assembled in the forecourt of the Villa Ruspoli, before passing by the lovely Paola Fountain and then driving down the slope of the Janiculum, looked highly distinguished in this timeless setting meant ever since antiquity for great showy processions. Rome is probably the only capital in the world where such a display does not appear anachronistic. As we crossed the Tiber and drove through Corso Vittorio-Emmanuele, Piazza Venezia, and Via Nazionale toward the Quirinal's plaza, Marini-Clarelli told me about his visit to Romania the preceding year, when he was part of the Italian delegation representing his monarch at the funeral of our Queen Marie.

At exactly eleven o'clock, our procession entered under the vault of the Quirinal. An honor guard of *bersaglieri* presented arms, footmen wearing the livery of Savoy opened the carriage doors and lowered the folding steps. We ascended the great staircase over which rises the wall into which is embedded the famous fresco by Melozzo da Forli, a fragment of the larger work that adorned the nearby Church of the Holy Apostles before it caught fire. On the top step another master of ceremonies, Prince Ruffo di Calabria, greeted me and ushered me through a magnificent hall hung with Gobelin tapestries, which one would have liked to admire at greater leisure, onward between two rows of palace guards in their red uniforms and shining helmets, into a first chamber where Count de Sant'Elia, grand master of ceremonies, was waiting. We all then moved into a second chamber where members of the Royal Household were introduced to me. Sant'Elia entered the throne room to announce my arrival. I walked in alone. The king came toward me—smiling, amiable, very direct—and held out his hand with a few words of welcome. I gave him the letter in which my monarch appointed me as envoy extraordinary and minister plenipotentiary.

Our conversation began with social news. The king asked about our royal family and reminisced about his voyage to Romania in early 1894 as Prince of Piedmont. I was hard put for a rejoinder, since that was before my birth. He also spoke to me of our King Carol I ("a handsome presence"), but not of his present successor, Carol II. He complained of feeling his years: when one has reached seventy, that's a rather long life! I replied that he wore his years lightly, and that because he could proudly look back upon his reign as one distinguished by four victorious wars and an unmatched time of prosperity for his country; moreover, a wise foreign policy kept Italy at peace in the midst of nations that were tearing one another apart.

I added that his people and other peace-loving nations would be grateful to him down the years. The king smiled slightly—with skepticism: "You are telling me very kind things, my dear envoy, yet my reign is less filled with glory than you so courteously say. If we have had some successes over the years, believe me, it was not on account of me but thanks to circumstances. Even a mediocre individual may benefit from external events, and then it is claimed that it was through his own merit. If there is any merit to be found, it's that of my government. It would be a different story if things were going badly. When things go ill, then indeed, it's the monarchs who get blamed! As for maintaining peace, which gladdens you as it does us all, I can promise you that we will do our best to preserve it in the future too. One never knows what the future holds in store, but for the time being, as you can see, we go about our business in Italy without engaging in high politics."

I ventured to ask the king whether the new dedication of his people to hard work, and their patriotic self-discipline and restraint, came from their having willingly abandoned their destiny into the hands of men they judge worthy of such trust. On the lips of my royal interlocutor there once again appeared a refined, skeptical smile, the same slightly ironic smile that one sees in certain old portraits of the House of Savoy. "But why should the leaders be the only ones to engage in politics? Every individual has a mind and the right to judge events and express opinions. From divergent opinions come useful debates, which then produce the good decision one ought to follow."

We talked about communism. There was a risk that this doctrine would infiltrate the Balkans as a result of Pan-Slavist affinities. Duty obliged me to point out that, more than ever, it was Romania's role to serve as a dike or barrier. And a dike needs to be strengthened, not weakened. We are sometimes told that one dike can be replaced by another. It seemed to me, nevertheless, that the first or farthest out dike was the most vital. The king agreed with me. "To be sure," he said, "a barrier is only useful if it is strong. And I fear more a peaceful infiltration, which is difficult to combat, than I do a military move that one can resist with arms. Speak to Ciano along those lines. The role of a diplomatic agent can be very important. When I was young, I thought diplomats were pretty useless. . . . " I dared interrupt him: "Quite a few diplomats share that opinion, Sire!" The king began to laugh: "You're not allowing me to finish my thought. Now that I'm old, I've come to the conclusion that an envoy who is bright, serious, and active can turn a situation fully around."

We ended by speaking about Romano-Hungarian relations—of course! The king said he knew that during my appointment in Budapest I tried to smooth out harsh edges and that a détente ensued. I drew his attention to measures recently taken by my government to improve even further the situation of ethnic minorities. "That's the right idea," he said, "try to conciliate them. One can't be enemies forever." I echoed his sentiments, but I asked for Italy's assistance in making Budapest duly appreciate our efforts—that is, by persuading our Hungarian neighbors that fostering a mood of good relations between them and us was vital, and that our petty quarrels had to be set aside at all costs, in light of the grave common problems that faced us. "Your border with Russia is, I believe, much longer than the Russian-Hungarian border," the king noted. I concurred, adding, "All the same, Sire, their border is wide enough to allow subversive doctrines to filter in, and if our border with Russia is vaster yet, that is all the more reason for everyone to pitch in and help to reinforce that line separating two ideologies, instead of weakening it." After this exchange, I introduced my staff to the king, and then we returned to the legation in the same ceremonial fashion as we had left.

Next I was greeted by the Prince of Piedmont, and my wife and I were welcomed by Queen Helena. And then there were wreaths to place in the Pantheon before the tombs of Victor Emmanuel II and Umberto I, as well as at the Altar of the Fatherland before the tomb of the unknown soldier. Once all these rites had been performed, I had been well and truly anointed envoy to the court of Italy. All that remained for me to do was to become *Romano di Roma* by paying a visit in the Capitol to the governor of the Eternal City, Prince Gian-Giacomo Borghese, who offered me a large plot within the land zoned for the 1942 World Fair in Rome, in order to accommodate the Romanian pavilion. I accepted, of course, without voicing my doubts about the feasibility of that grand project. Poor "E42," as it was nicknamed by the Romans: it was a dream that never materialized, but its preparations cost Italian taxpayers vast amounts.

Only once, during my short appointment in Rome, was I received by Mussolini (on February 16, 1940). He did not let the meeting overstep the confines of a polite social conversation, for he said that exchanges of views with foreign envoys were a job he left to Ciano.

FOREIGN COLLEAGUES IN ROME

André François-Poncet, the French ambassador in Rome, sent word that he would like to be in contact with me even before I had presented my credentials to the king, which was the investiture of a head envoy. I therefore went to the marvelous Palazzo Farnese, which in earlier years had lodged many kings and was now the residence of the embassy of France. Located within a poor popular neighborhood, the strong yet restrained façade designed by Antonio Sangallo struck one as a haughty contrast with its humble surroundings. From their windows up high, the envoys of the Third Republic impassively observed the anti-French demonstrations organized from time to time by the Fascist authorities. My car glided in beneath the noble arches. I climbed the great staircase, one of the grandest built in the Renaissance, which leads you right up to the Farnese Hercules. From that spot, a young embassy secretary led me down a gallery as broad as a boulevard, to a door on the right that was crested by a cardinal's hat, emblem of Alessandro Farnese. I entered into the ambassador's beautiful personal office. In the seat that the first time I visited this office had been occupied by Barrère, a man courteous in manners but with a cold gaze, as piercing as a steel blade, I now found a lively and affable man, full of vigor. A glint in the eyes, a small mustache, a bow tie: that's all I noticed at first. It was André François-Poncet. He was highly intelligent and had great wit—a bit more, they say, than touchy Fascists could stand! Previously, he had done a brilliant job as ambassador in Berlin: even though the Hitler regime incited many delicate situations, he gained authority and won the esteem of many in power. Transferred to Rome on the eve of the great conflict, he took up his new post under circumstances that were far from auspicious. I cannot write his name without immediately recalling his friendly support and the valuable information he generously passed on to me during our overlapping years in the Eternal City. During many a lively conversation, sparkling with wit, his level-headed views neatly put into perspective any wild rumor or other that was spreading through the chancelleries of certain colleagues.

On the day we first met, he showed his skepticism about the peaceful intents that Ciano had voiced to me. He believed that the "father-in-law" was far too enterprising and enamored of his interventionist doctrine ever to settle for a permanent neutrality, even if that was a fruitful option for Italy. Mussolini, he said, was beset with regrets, for he had in effect given his word to Hitler. His secret fear was to witness his country doing the same about-face as in 1915, which he thought would fully disgrace it in the eyes of posterity. It was true that neither the king, nor the field marshals, nor public opinion, wanted to go to war against the Allies. All the same, François-Poncet said, the Duce was always capable of a surprise. Ah, he sighed, if only one could offer Mussolini a neutral Balkan group, over which he might fancy to preside, as a stage and as an outlet for his unspent energies! That would be a service rendered to everyone. For that to happen, however, the Danubian countries would first need to take serious steps on the economic front in order to convince Italy that it would be both prestigious and profitable for it to head their organization. In the meantime, Ciano continued to be very suspicious and worried about the Ankara pact, even though François-Poncet and his British colleague insisted that this agreement presented no threat to Italy. The two ambassadors entreated Ciano to join the pact, as a safeguard to the status quo in the Balkans. The hitch was that prior to that Rome would have to put aside its border revisionism.

I mentioned to François-Poncet rumors heard in Budapest about a possible German offensive against Romania. He too had got wind of it and had been authorized by his government to inform Palazzo Chigi that France and Britain would respect Italian neutrality and help to keep the peace in the Danube Basin, provided that no aggression took place in the Balkans. Whenever the opportunity occurred, he had reminded Ciano that an aggression against Romania or any other country in that region would automatically and swiftly call into play the Franco-Anglo-Turkish pledge and spark a general conflict in Southeastern Europe. A new "Salonika front" would be set up under Weygand's command, an idea endorsed by Prince-Regent Paul. In reply, Ciano always intimated that this was not the scenario Berlin had in mind: instead, the Germans hoped to pressure Bucharest from within the country itself. This did not mean that Mussolini would be opposed to sacrificing Romania's territorial interests in order to secure what he called a stable peace in Central Europe. Quite to the contrary.

In short, nothing allowed me to entertain optimistic thoughts as I left the Palazzo Farnese and my first meeting with a colleague in Rome.

I was to see fairly often Sir Percy Loraine, the very likable and tradition-conscious British ambassador. In his house I also met Lady Halifax. He was convinced that Mussolini intended to join the war on Hitler's side.

Phillips, the U.S. ambassador, struck me as a bright, refined man, quite "Old England" in style. He apparently hoped that the Italians, since they feared the Germans as much as they did the Allies, would stay put. That opinion was shared by Count Kerchove de Denterghem, the friendly and voluble Belgian ambassador. He remained very confident that Ciano, who had made it into high society, was put off by Hitler's crass proletarians.

One of the most agreeable conversationalists among the foreign diplomats in Rome was Helfant, the Soviet chargé d'affaires. He was a Jew with a supple, brilliant mind, a refined, likable fellow—a bit boastful, and even something of a snob. His communist feelings must not have been too deeply seated or strong. Indeed, they were to melt in the Roman sun: upon being recalled to Moscow, he chose to go to the United States, where he was said to have a dentist brother, and he settled there, quite indifferent to Moscow's fulminations.

The first time he came to visit he confided to me that he was a close friend of Ciano's, whom he saw at least once a week until the Finnish crisis. He avowed being on such warm terms with the foreign minister that he had been so bold as to advise him not to wear his fascist cap so low over one eye, since that made him look rather "dense" [*sic*], that is to say, not quite up to snuff as chief of the Fascist foreign service. Even assuming the veracity of this avowal, it should be noted that Helfant's good advice fell on deaf ears, for Ciano kept right on wearing his cap at an angle.

Helfant also claimed to me that he was a friend of Fascist Secretary-General Muti, which seemed rather improbable, since Muti was renowned for his violently anti-Communist views and for the role he had played against the "reds" in the Spanish Civil War. When I told him that I too was acquainted with Muti and that we had paid each other mutual visits, Helfant pulled a wry, slightly disdainful face: "What," he exclaimed, "Muti now pays calls on envoys, even though he is still so crass and uncultured?" I could not help smiling, in secret at least, at this rather unexpected remark on the part of a Bolshevik. We spoke about politics. He considered Ciano less pro-German after the dressing-down he received from Hitler at Berchtesgaden the previous summer, but all the same not brave enough to oppose his father-in-law's pro-Axis policies. In order to tighten the bonds between Italy and the Balkans, Ciano was willing to practice intrigue: thus, in the case of Romania, he wanted to delude people into thinking that it would be attacked by Russia, which was totally untrue. I replied that there was only one remedy: let Moscow through real deeds demonstrate to us its good intentions.

My round of visits took me to Hüseyin Ragip Baydur, Turkey's charming ambassador, a bright, lively, refined man whom I first met when he was envoy in Bucharest, from where he was then transferred to Moscow. The latter post is probably where he acquired habits of utmost prudence: he used to close all the doors of his personal office and spoke in whispers to his visitors. According to him, the autumn military maneuvers had brought to light great armament gaps in the Italian army. The Duce had called to task Pariani, undersecretary of war, who in turn blamed Finance Minister Guarnieri, saying he had not provided the necessary foreign exchange. End result, both men paid the piper: they were dismissed from their posts. That was also why Victor Emmanuel III had succeeded in prescribing a "non-belligerence" policy. In retaliation, Mussolini appointed as chief of staff Field Marshal Graziani, whom the king liked far less than Badoglio.

Our Yugoslav colleague, Bočko Cristić, was quite pessimistic. Withdrawn and close-lipped, he was in the dumps in his sumptuous drawing rooms at the Palazzo Borghese. He foresaw Poland's permanent demise and Germany's victory. The present state of relations between Italy and Turkey looked ominous to him, and he did not believe that a neutral bloc could be created in the Balkans: "That would be another aberration along the lines of the Little Entente." Being a hypersensitive person, he could not take his mind off the present-day slaughters and destruction, nor could he rid himself of the foreboding that all these calamities would sooner or later befall his own homeland. In spite of the happy family life that he led, with a charming wife from Montenegro and beautiful children, two years later he could no longer endure the misfortunes of his country and he took his own life while in exile in Switzerland.

My Hellenic colleague Petros Metaxas, future envoy of Greece in France and then in Switzerland, had already been in residence in Rome for nine years when I arrived there. He was the doyen of foreign envoys at the court of Italy and presided at our weekly dinners in the Albergo Quirinale. Refined, bright, and a perfect gentleman, he was well assisted by his wife and daughters. Even though Italo-Greek relations were never easy, he had built up an excellent situation in Rome. He complained about how difficult it was to obtain reliable information in a garrulous country, where only those who know anything for certain keep their mouths shut. In Palazzo Chigi, he groaned, Buti (the political director) had not a clue about state secrets, whereas Vitelli and Anfuso, Ciano's pals, were as mute as fish. Rome and Athens had recently exchanged diplomatic notes as an intended transition from the 1928 Italian-Greek pact of conciliation and arbitration, now about to expire, toward a new agreement that was to be negotiated when peace resumed. Yet Metaxas displayed a certain skepticism regarding this exchange of notes. While the Fascist press wanted to view this as a tangible warming of relations between the two countries—perhaps still with an eye toward creating a neutral Balkan bloc—my Greek colleague believed that it was "much ado about nothing." Future events were to prove him right.

The German ambassador in Rome was Hans-Georg von Mackensen, son of the old field marshal and son-in-law of Baron Konstantin von Neurath (former ambassador to Italy and to Britain, and later foreign minister). We had known each other at two earlier points in our careers: the first time as mission secretaries also in Rome, the second time as envoys in Budapest. Now, in 1939, he had just returned from Berlin when I paid my first call. Our conversation turned naturally and very promptly to the subject of the Balkans. He assured me that Hitler was firmly committed to maintaining peace there, for economic reasons at the very least. He added that Stalin's intentions were much the same, and he offered as proof the reassuring declarations spontaneously made by the USSR to Romania. "There is no question at all of reopening the Bessarabian question," asserted Mackensen, even though he had in fact been informed of the secret Germano-Russian protocol that granted Moscow a free hand in that ancient Romanian province. "If any malicious rumors have reached you on this score," he continued, "they can only come from enemies of Germany who hope to see the conflict widen." And Mackensen sought to convince me that the only dark cloud on the horizon in the Balkans was the tripartite Ankara pact and the Franco-British security pledges extended to Romania and Greece. I tried in vain to point out that all these diplomatic agreements were purely defensive in intent, and that if only Germany and Italy were to join in, they would bolster the neutrality of Southeastern Europe. Mackensen stuck to the official line of the Wilhelmstrasse and Palazzo Chigi, asserting that those were scheming maneuvers by Britain, whose Intelligence Service had just engineered in Munich the failed assassination attempt against the Führer, and that Mussolini would never place himself at the head of a neutral Balkan organization in which enemies of the Axis could act as they pleased. He added that thanks to the numerous submarines being built, Germany would destroy Britain's commercial fleet and bring England to its knees.

✧ ✧ ✧

This round of courtesy calls was interrupted by an unforgettable visit of several days to Sicily, where my wife christened the Romanian ship *Mangalia*, ordered from Palermo's shipyards. While there I went to pay my respects to N. Bălcescu's tomb. I shall never forget the charming welcome extended to us by Palermo's society (especially Prince and Princess di Mirto in their beautiful Palazzo San Marco), nor the dream towns of Monreale and Taormina.

One of my most congenial colleagues was the Portuguese envoy, Lobo d'Avila Lima. Unfortunately one saw little of him, for he spent the better part of his time in Paris. He even explained to me the scheme that he had devised in order to stay in Paris without relinquishing his post: officially he went off to San Remo (located on Italian territory), there he unobtrusively "slipped aboard a bus to Nice," whence a "little sleeping car" on a train sped him to Paris, and no one, thought he, was the wiser for it. With a sigh I had to inform this friendly colleague that my work load at the legation and the numerous compatriots who came through Rome were the reason I could not, for my part, adopt his scheme.

THE "NEUTRAL BLOC"

The notion of bringing a group of countries in the southeast of Europe together into a neutral bloc centered around Italy seemed to Romania a rather appealing idea in those opening months of World War II. Such an organization would have several aims: to maintain a perfect neutrality throughout the conflict; to deter acts of aggression between member states; to ensure that any member state "subjected to an external attack" would at least benefit from the amicable neutrality of the other member states; to regulate in amicable fashion the presence of military forces along shared borders; to maintain friendly and permanent contacts among respective governments; and finally to establish an economic order in conformity with the interests of all states that signed the agreement. The creation of such a bloc would have helped the Fascist government of Italy to maintain its neutrality, or rather its status of nonbelligerence, in the face of possible pressures and threats exerted by its Axis partner. It would also, in the felicitous words of François-Poncet, "offer Mussolini a political platform and an outlet for his unspent energies." Moreover, such an organization would usefully keep in check the revisionist tendencies of Hungary and Bulgaria, two countries harnessed for the time being to a peaceful coach led by the Duce. That was also the reason Italy's participation was so necessary. Without it Budapest and Sofia would both reckon that they were being hoodwinked, and would never willingly enter into an arrangement that would look to them like a trap set by the Balkan Entente.

As I pointed out earlier, the French ambassador in Rome had perfectly understood this point of view, and he recommended it to the Quai d'Orsay. However, his colleagues elsewhere did not all share that opinion. While the French ambassadors in Bucharest and Belgrade concurred with him, those in Athens and Ankara voiced some skepticism. In Massigli's opinion, the neutral bloc became pointless once Italy was included. Berlin wanted a neutral Hungary and Bulgaria; as long as that was so, both countries would have to pursue the same neutral course as the Balkan Entente, and for that reason there was no need to create such an ephemeral bloc: the day Germany or Russia decided to launch an offensive toward the southeast, nothing would be left of that celebrated bloc. This hard-nosed outlook seemed to prevail in the French foreign ministry, where many claimed to be for a neutral Balkan area but against Italy's participation in a neutral bloc within that region. Perhaps these conflicting views gave pause to François-Poncet, for he eventually showed some hesitations about a bloc that might become "manipulated" by Rome.

That thesis was not accepted in London, though the Quai d'Orsay intimated it was. On the contrary, in London it was thought that Italy had to be included in any concerted effort that countries of Southeastern Europe undertook to keep their region out of the war. The only stipulation requested by the Foreign Office was the prior assent of Turkey, complete and with no reservations, since an Italian "chairmanship" would produce alarm in Ankara.

Yet the Turkish government did not appear at all worried. Its only fears were that Sofia and Budapest might try to "negotiate" before joining the bloc—in order to win special advantages detrimental to other countries that signed on—and also that the proposed pact might turn into a purely symbolic gesture of collaboration, for it remained vague about the specific aid that would be furnished to a member state when it became the victim of external aggression. The Turkish government declared, however, that it "accepted favorably any initiative apt to prevent the present conflict from spreading," and it pointed to the like-minded pact that it had just signed with Britain and France. Hence it stated that no difficulty was seen on the Turkish side, nor any obstacle that might hinder the realization of this project, which the Turkish government would strive to assist. Nevertheless, the Turkish ambassador, Ragip Baydur, privately confided to me his lack of enthusiasm for a bloc that might fall under the sway of Italy.

Athens, too, was determined "to encourage any initiative aimed at limiting the present conflict, and to greet with favor any effort leading to trust as well as to organizing the security of neighboring countries, with an eye to preventing war within those regions." The Greek side was "happy to lend its support toward the realization of the project in question," but wished, of course, to avoid an Italian "chairmanship."

Yugoslavia was even more worried by Italy's inclusion in the neutral bloc. By no means would it hear of an Italian "chairmanship" or "leadership," even though my colleague Cristić conceded that such an organization of states needed the support of a major military power. The Belgrade government was also inclined to think that this organization could not take shape before several thorny problems had been resolved, among which it cited Turko-Italian relations and the need to ease tensions with Bulgaria and Hungary. That being said, Yugoslavia was "happy to grant her approval and support to the project."

What, however, was Rome's opinion of the project? Mussolini had been hesitant ever since the signing of the Anglo-Franco-Turkish pact; he wanted to see first what stance Turkey would take following this "enhancement of prestige." If Turkey grew too strong, the Duce would be denied his wish, which was to be the leading player within the neutral bloc, and that was the only role that could offer a true political advantage for him. Above all, he did not want to take the initiative, out of fear that a setback would sully his personal prestige. That explained Ciano's noncommittal posture when he spoke to me about this matter. The Duce would have felt more trustful if the neutral Balkan bloc had expanded into a neutral Mediterranean bloc that included Franco's Spain. Virginio Gayda, who in his *Giornale d'Italia* editorials acted as spokesman for the Palazzo Chigi, confided to me the worries instilled in Rome by Turkey's foreign policy: the presence of the Ankara government would be the chief obstacle to creating a neutral bloc, for it would serve as the British cabinet's broker in order to lure Italy into the Allies' game plan. Italy was not seeking to head the bloc, but neither should it forget that it had become the major power in the Balkans. (Always the same bromide!)

In short, the inclusion of three countries benefiting from the Franco-British guarantees—Romania, Greece, and especially Turkey—looked ominous to Mussolini and Ciano, who would certainly have preferred a web of separate bilateral agreements with each of the Balkan states, which would have enabled Italy to set preconditions in each case. This would have been especially pleasing to Csáky, who, in agreement with Ciano, had just given a speech to put conditions before Romania.

Germany, for its part, would have accepted the inclusion of Turkey in the neutral group only if Ankara had first "clarified" its stance vis-à-vis the Axis.

✧ ✧ ✧

In the meantime, an important reshuffling of the Fascist government was under way. On October 31, several officials were shunted aside, among others: Alfieri, General Pariani, and the ineffable Starace, called the regime's dumbest man: "*La lupa è vorace, l'aquila rapace, l'oca Starace.*"[3]

[3]"The wolf is voracious, the eagle rapacious, the goose truly Staracius."

Among their colleagues they had been considered the most pro-German. Did their departure signify that the Duce wanted to give his cabinet a less Axis-like profile, so as to facilitate the role he hoped to play in the neutral bloc? In any case, those who replaced them were for the most part associates of Ciano's, whose allegiance to Germany was less firm. Field Marshal Graziani, now head of the chiefs of staff, had allegedly opposed the German alliance, which is perhaps why Mussolini frowned on him for quite a while. As for Ettore Muti, the party's new secretary-general, only one thing was known about that young man: he fought fanatically in Spain against the "reds." It seemed unlikely, therefore, that he would be fond of the Reich, a current ally of the Kremlin. I had lunch that very day with Princess Maria of Greece and the François-Poncets. The French ambassador as well as the princess and her husband, Admiral Ioannides, agreed that the cabinet reshuffle was a "change of tack in direction of the Western powers." However, added François-Poncet, it was best not to shout it from the rooftops, for fear of triggering an opposite reaction.

What seemed significant, however, was the renewal of economic negotiations between Italy and France, which were expected to result in new sales for Italian industries, totaling around one billion lire for orders of trucks, train cars, machine guns, anti-tank defenses, planes, and so on, with the raw materials being furnished by France. There was talk of similar negotiations with Britain. Italian industry would thus be snared with Allied manufacturing orders and, to that extent, prevented from working for Germany's benefit. But would Hitler allow his obedient sidekick to bolster in this way Britain's blockade of Germany? Nevertheless these factors, along with the exchange of diplomatic notes between Rome and Athens, left the door open for certain hopes—or should we say for questionable illusions?

✧ ✧ ✧

The thorniest Balkan policy issue facing Mussolini at that time was undoubtedly his relations with Greece. That large stumbling block needed to be overcome to pave the way for the creation of a neutral bloc in Southeastern Europe.

By seizing Albania, Italy had also become a Balkan power, and even the biggest Balkan power, as Ciano loved to proclaim, he having engineered the shameful coup that plucked the Skipetar kingdom. Nor was he inclined to stop there. He hoped to push on, perhaps as far as Salonika.

He thought he could get his way more easily by means of peaceful infiltration than by a military operation—always hazardous for Italy, as future events would demonstrate, especially once the German military forces lost interest in the Danube Basin, being bent on ruling only the continent's northern zones. Hence, the necessity for Italy of finding a modus vivendi with Greece.

Relations between Rome and Athens had had their highs and their lows since the famous Corfu incident of 1923. Yet on September 23, 1928, after many arduous negotiations, the two governments had managed to sign in Rome a pact of friendship, conciliation, and arbitration in keeping with trusty old principles of the League of Nations. This event succeeded in calming the general mood but not for long, since the Abyssinian sanctions and war sparked new tensions between Rome and Athens, suspected by Italy of following Britain's lead. Tensions worsened when the Fascist power annexed Albania, and that obliged Mussolini to take a clear stand. He accordingly chose the peaceful option.

Looking at Albania, the Greeks were understandably worried about the concentration of Italian troops there, and Athens rightly viewed it as a sign of aggressive intentions in regard to Salonika, whose broader frame was the great European war under way. In order to alleviate this justifiable anxiety, Fornari, the Italian chargé d'affaires in Athens (and later ambassador in Paris), was instructed by his government to ply General Metaxas, the Greek premier, with requisite pledges of peace.

On April 11, 1939, he acquitted himself of that task by assuring the head of state, to whom he had been accredited by the Duce himself, of Italy's good intentions: "Any rumor heard now or at a later date concerning an alleged military move by Italy against Greece is entirely false and can only be the work of agents provocateurs. Fascist Italy confirms once more its firm intention of respecting in an absolute way the territorial integrity of the Greek mainland and islands. Fascist Italy wishes to maintain and expand the cordial relations binding the two countries. It is also willing to demonstrate this in tangible ways."

The following day this declaration was made public through an official announcement, and the Greek envoy conveyed to the Palazzo Chigi Premier Metaxas's thanks. Metaxas was, he said, "persuaded that no event could ever trouble the traditional friendship [*sic*] existing between the two countries." He rejoiced that "new foundations were being laid to ensure a new period of friendship and peaceful partnership." Furthermore, once war had broken out in Europe, a joint communiqué issued on September 20 both in Rome and Athens "happily took note of the complete trust that continued to underpin the friendly and sincere relations between the two countries." It further noted "the tangible demonstration of these sentiments by the decision of the Italian government to withdraw its military forces from the Greek-Albanian border and by similar measures taken by the Greek government."

It must nevertheless be observed that this exchange of cordial gestures was underscored more vigorously in Rome than in Athens, where a certain skepticism continued to prevail. Since General Metaxas appeared in no hurry to conclude a new pact while war continued and Italy's stance remained unclear, it was decided not to proceed beyond an exchange of diplomatic notes, on September 30, which reaffirmed the principles set forth in the expired pact and employed flowery speech that was, alas, as short-lived as eloquent: "Italy's friendly predisposition toward Greece," "the cordial mood binding the two countries," "a new period of friendship, common understanding, and growing mutual trust," "hope that the international situation will evolve in ways that soon offer both governments the opportunity to firm up their relations in ways that will foster a fruitful and trusting partnership in all areas."

Is it surprising that people everywhere were growing a bit distrustful of statesmen's rhetorical flourishes?

✧ ✧ ✧

What, I believe, finally put an end to the project of a neutral bloc was Mackensen's formal declaration to me on November 22, 1939, that Germany would categorically oppose any act that, under the appearance of neutrality, might be aimed against it, and that it would prevent Italy, Hungary, and Bulgaria from taking part in it. Since Csáky, at the prompting of his Axis friends, had just delivered a speech demanding concessions from Romania, the German ambassador had no difficulty in demonstrating to me that his protégés would obey him quick as a wink. I tried one final assault by asking, "What if Italy were to join the neutral bloc in spite of your predictions?" "Even in that case, we would oppose it," Mackensen replied without the slightest hesitation. I understood at once that he had received official instructions from Berlin to sabotage the neutral bloc.

All this did not deter Ciano from dreaming of a rapprochement with certain Balkan countries by means of bilateral agreements. To François-Poncet he boasted of his warm relations with Hungary—he went so far as to speak of a possible personal union after Horthy—and even with Bulgaria: relations with Yugoslavia and Greece were also improving. Only about Romania and Turkey did he remain silent—in Romania's case because he endorsed plans to revise Romania's borders, and in Turkey's case because he considered that it paid complete allegiance to the Franco-British alliance. Sir Percy Loraine told me that Italy felt unsure about the degree of complicity between Germany and Russia, and so preferred to stand aside from any association that might displease either Berlin or Moscow.

The reason the Fascist regime so strongly supported Hungary's border revisionism had its origin twelve years earlier. Italy had emerged from World War I with a severe inferiority complex, and ever since it had yearned to pass truly for a great power in the eyes of international public opinion. Above all it needed "satellites," which, like a seawall, would hold back the German drive into Central Europe and further Italy's aspirations in that region. In 1926 when General Averescu came to power in Romania, Mussolini had hoped to turn the Latin country at the mouth of the Danube into the hub of his diplomatic operations in Southeastern Europe. A pact was agreed upon to that effect and solemnly signed in Rome.

Unfortunately for the Duce, the Averescu government suffered from shallow roots: it fell in 1927, and with it vanished the Palazzo Chigi's hopes of seeing Romania relinquish Yugoslavia and the Little Entente allied to France. Fascist Italy had to cast around for another "pawn" through which to pursue its political ends in the East. During a visit to Rome, Count Bethlen made himself available and, moreover, offered himself without any preconditions. Hungary became not only the Duce's most obedient satellite but also the keystone of the short-lived "Rome-Vienna-Budapest triangle." All Hungary asked for was that its territorial demands against its neighbors be taken seriously and be supported from Italy's eminent stage as a major power. That is precisely what the orator on the balcony of Palazzo Venezia delivered, along with loud bluster and needless hostility. Yet Italy's Magyarophile policy secretly irritated Hitler a bit, for he felt that it was aimed against his own aspirations in Southeastern Europe. I say "a bit" because the Nazi government knew that, for geographic reasons, Hungary remained in the Reich's sphere of influence, and that if Budapest were absolutely forced to choose between Berlin and Rome, it would side with Berlin and not Rome. Horthy, too, knew that and consequently sought to avoid the dilemma altogether. Mussolini and Ciano were the only ones capable of imagining that Hungary might ever afford the luxury of taking a stance against Germany. However, since that fantasy was firmly embedded in their minds, they dismissed the idea that a neutral bloc could take shape in Southeastern Europe without a territorial readjustment that would satisfy (at least to some extent) the Hungarians, who dreamed of St. Stephen's crown and who heaped compliments on them.

On November 30, I had a long meeting with Ciano regarding this matter. He expressed satisfaction about declarations made by Tătărescu, the new Romanian prime minister, and by Gafencu, the foreign minister, whose remarks on Italy had been greeted with applause in the Chamber of Deputies. He did not conceal his pleasure that Gafencu, while taking issue with Csáky's charges, did not launch a polemic against his Hungarian counterpart. While on that topic, he wished to deny all allegations that the speech given by the Hungarian foreign minister had been submitted to him beforehand for his authorization. On the contrary, he assured me, he was always pleading for moderation from Budapest. What honeyed blarney!

In conclusion, the project for a neutral bloc in the Balkans came to nothing. Germany's opposition, the inclusion of Turkey, the British pledges to Romania and Greece, the diverging aspirations of the states in Southeastern Europe were not the only reasons why the plan fell through. There was also the Duce's unwillingness to join an association of neutral states, since he was tacitly determined to enter into the war at a later date. It might be in his interest some day to attack the very Balkan states whose territorial integrity he was being asked to guarantee, and he wanted to have a free hand for that. In the words of Ambassador Buti, the Palazzo Chigi's political director, "Italy is resolved to take no steps toward organizing a neutral bloc that it did not want to join and that could not come into being without it."

✧ ✧ ✧

On December 16, 1939, Ciano gave one of his "great speeches," as a show of his independence. He pretended to complain about Hitler. He recalled that upon signing the "Iron Pact" Germany had pledged, along with Italy, to remain at peace for at least three years "and not to disturb it through threatening or aggressive postures." And yet, it was only at 10:00 P.M. on August 22, and over the telephone, that he learned that a German-Soviet nonaggression pact would be signed the very next day.

Ciano even paid homage to Poland's heroism, although he added that the "expansion of the Polish state" beyond its ethnic limits had been devised only "for the purpose of encircling the Reich." Finally he spoke disapprovingly of projects to establish blocs of neutral countries. Italy's relations with Balkan countries did not require "new sets of regulations." He listed the excellent relations that Italy enjoyed with those several states. For the first time he voiced a few amiable words about Romania, for which I went over to his office and thanked him.

Italy's goal, as Sir Percy Loraine observed to me, seemed to consist in securing a free hand in the Balkans and playing there the role of referee. Its desire was to exclude both Germany and Russia from that region. During a dinner at our legation, Federzoni took the opportunity to say to me, "Do give up this idea of a neutral Balkan bloc, which is so vexing to Berlin and pointless too, from the Italian point of view, after Ciano's recent speech, which proclaimed our good relations with every country of Southeastern Europe."

II. 1940

In the last days of autumn 1939, it was difficult to imagine that Italy, although it claimed to be a neutral or nonbelligerent country, could indefinitely remain on the sidelines of a major European war without risking the same fate as Spain or Sweden in earlier centuries and dwindling into a second-rate power. A permanent state of neutrality seemed all the more implausible considering that the Fascist government made no secret of its boundless ambitions and that fascist doctrine advocated policies of direct action in internal as well as external matters.

ITALY'S STANCE IN THE WAR

Mussolini reckoned that he would have a major and decisive say when the future peace was concluded. He did not want a repetition of Versailles, and he made no bones about it: that is to say, he ruled out any future peace arrangement reached without taking the wishes of Italy into account. Neither would he allow that the Mediterranean question be settled without his input. In short, there were only two paths to achieving his ends. The first was an armed intervention, unleashed at the most opportune moment, so as to contribute to the victor's success and thereby entitle Mussolini to grab what he coveted. The second road was to maintain a nonbelligerent stance until the end of the war, but only on the basis of a prior agreement that would recognize the validity of Italy's demands.

To ready the first option—armed intervention—the Fascist government was already making all requisite military preparations: rearming, reshuffling the top staff, conditioning public opinion through warlike speeches. However, with respect to the second path, the Duce and his son-in-law were still hesitant: in order to initiate even secret discussions toward a fruitful option of nonbelligerence, they still needed to obtain a clearer view of their partner's game plan. It was crucial not to tip one's hand too soon. It seemed wiser to bide one's time until the Allies and the Germans had their first big clashes, since the war's prelude—the *phony war,* called in Italy *la guerra non guerregiata*—did not yet yield enough clues with which to gauge accurately the relative power of each side. Mussolini wanted to make his decision known neither too soon (for fear of making a bad call), nor too late (for fear of being by then no longer needed as an ally). His sympathies, nevertheless, were clearly on the side of the "have nots," that is to say of Germany, whose victory would have opened for him immense vistas of colonial expansion. Moreover, he would have thought it an enduring honor to rewrite the course of Italy's twentieth-century history by bringing about a switch of alliances reversing the switch performed in 1915. "Had I held power in 1915," he confided to Count Csáky, "I would not have allowed our weapons to be turned against our allies." His declaration was rather odd, for in those earlier days he was in the ranks of the Socialist party and was calling for war against Germany and Austria-Hungary.

"Italy outside the fray but not above it": that was the slogan proposed by Senator Maurizio Maraviglia. "Our neutrality is not permanent . . . Italy cannot be indifferent to the fate of Europe. We keep our weapons at the ready. . . . We will stay at peace as long as Italy's best interests continue to be respected and adequately served." There were endless rumors heard to the effect that the Duce intended to relinquish neutrality in order to enter the lists at Germany's side. The king was said to oppose that plan with all his might. Italian soldiers, disguised as workers, were allegedly being sent by ship from Bari to Albania. Public opinion was being prepared for war. Muti, the party's secretary-general, was instructed to deliver speeches that demonstrated how Italy's best interests lay on the German side, and Virginio Gayda discussed and elaborated the same idea in the *Giornale d'Italia.* Several factors appeared to corroborate the convergence of interests between Germany and Italy: economic tensions that set Rome at odds with London and Paris (Mussolini was loath to furnish military supplies to the Allies, and the British threatened to intercept German coal shipments to Italy), fierce protests by the government, conclusion of an economic agreement between Germany and Italy, a propaganda campaign in the press. Furthermore, neither François-Poncet nor Sir Percy Loraine had any illusions on this score. According to the latter, the most recent exchange of diplomatic notes between Rome and London "reeks of vitriol."

Eager to compromise Mussolini for good, here came Ribbentrop, arriving in Rome on the spur of the moment on March 9, 1940, with a large retinue (a total of thirty-five people). Since Hitler distrusted Ciano on account of his more conciliatory attitude toward the Allies, he dispatched his loyal henchman to speak directly to the Duce. Their task, it was believed, was to draw up together the demands of the Axis, which were to be submitted to Sumner Welles, in case peace discussions took place. The agenda might also have included how to foster a Rome-Moscow rapprochement and how to weave even tighter bonds within the Germano-Italian alliance.

With respect to Sumner Welles's mission, that envoy had found during his first trip through Rome that Mussolini was as intensely pro-German as he was anti-Russian. Phillips, the American ambassador, told me that Welles had not been pleased with that initial contact, which had confined itself to a review of the concessions demanded by the "proletarian states," that is, the Axis powers.

The Italo-Russian rapprochement was an arduous project. On the evening of Ribbentrop's departure I dined with Mackensen at the Soviet embassy. The German ambassador kept praising the wisdom of the Latvians and Estonians—for they had given in to the Soviets—and blaming the Finns for their "stubbornness." What a strange discourse in the mouth of a former Prussian officer!

The outcome of Ribbentrop's discussions in Rome was summed up for me by François-Poncet in one sentence: "The Italians will join the war; it will be either in three days or in three months." It would appear, however, that there remained several unresolved questions preventing Mussolini and Ribbentrop from sealing their agreement, for only a few days after Ribbentrop's departure, the Duce and the Führer met at the Brenner Pass, on March 18. In diplomatic circles, many hypotheses were bandied around. Mostly it was thought that the Führer must have shared his military plans and, at the same time, must have assured the Duce that the USSR would attack neither Romania nor Hungary. Did Mussolini take the risk of proposing a peace plan to his fearsome partner, as thought the Soviet chargé d'affaires, Helfant? Who can tell? Ciano had the decency to inform Sir Percy Loraine and François-Poncet that the Brenner meeting signaled a strengthening of the Axis.

The occupation of Denmark and Norway by German military forces on April 9, 1940, naturally boosted Hitler's prestige in Italy. Political moderates feared that this would go to Mussolini's head and prompt him to make a military or naval move. On the day that followed this new Nazi onslaught, Ciano queried François-Poncet, "Well, why is it that the Germans always score points and the Allies miss theirs?" The Duce, for his part, declared on that very day to a delegation of disabled veterans: "We will wage war when the time is right, we will indeed. Any Italian who does not consider this an ironclad necessity should take off his fascist beret and don a doorman's cap. Are we to become a mere tourist haven like Switzerland?" Other members of the cabinet used the same pitch during their meetings with me. The press tried to arouse public opinion against the Allies, and despite the sweet Roman springtime the air smelled of gunpowder.

On May 7, at a luncheon in the Belgian embassy, Mrs. Nieuwenhuys, wife of that country's ambassador to the Vatican, told me that government officials in Brussels expected that any day now the Germans would attack Belgium. That evening at the Villa Ruspoli I had dinner guests, both Italian and foreign. Colleagues included U.S. ambassador Phillips and Dutch envoy Hubrecht with their wives. The Italians were Prince and Princess Rofredo Caetani di Bassiano, Marquess and Marchioness Theodolo Theodoli, Count and Countess Giulio Macchi di Cellere, Countess Suardi, née Patrizi. They all seemed apprehensive about what tomorrow would bring. Phillips did not hide from me that the peace pledge given to him by Mussolini during their most recent meeting only concerned the short-term future. He was convinced that, if Germany attacked Belgium or the Netherlands, American public opinion would force the U.S. government to join the Allies at once in a war to liberate Europe, and he looked upon that war with some anxiety, given the numerical superiority of the German air force. "But still," he said, "we must keep all our confidence."

Sir Noel Charles, British chargé d'affaires, told me that he had seen Ciano and had asked him wryly, "Will you give us at least two weeks' notice before going over to our enemies?" To which the handsome Galeazzo had replied, with that expressive smile of his and several winks, "Don't worry, we're not thinking of going into action that fast!"

Those dodges fooled no one. Since the famous meeting at the Brenner Pass, the Italian government's behavior had clearly pointed to a slow but steady movement in the direction of active cooperation with its Axis ally. Military and economic preparations for going to war were being stepped up. Talk was all about military maneuvers on the Yugoslav border and naval maneuvers in the Ionian Sea. Mussolini was handing submarines over to Hitler, who in exchange was sending him Stukas. Army units in Albania were being reinforced in stages; two divisions had already left Bari toward Albanian ports. Four German military commissions were working around the clock in Rome, and all of Italy was swarming with Nazi servicemen, technicians, and "tourists."

Ribbentrop did not have great confidence in Mackensen, son-in-law of Neurath, whom he disliked. He had assigned him a minister-counsellor, Prince Otto von Bismarck, who (rightly or wrongly) was reputed to enjoy Ribbentrop's intimate trust and was meant to assist his chief in Rome and keep him under watch. It looks as though that trust was ill founded or but briefly justified, for Ciano's memoirs portray the Iron Chancellor's grandson as a decidedly lukewarm supporter of the regime he served.

Copies of the Duce's incendiary speeches were passed from hand to hand. "We must actively get ready to enter the war," he had allegedly told the disabled veterans' delegation on April 10, 1940. And later that month (April 21), while speaking to industrial federation presidents, he reportedly added, "We must go and fight if we don't want to waste a whole century in our national history!"

The mood reigning throughout the government clearly indicated that Italy was allowing itsef to slide into the war against France and Britain, and doing so in spite of her people's love of peace, in spite of the Vatican, in spite of the wishes of the royal house of Savoy.

Nonbelligerence was over. At hand now was "pre-belligerence," a term let loose by Maraviglia, budget chairman in the Senate. But Mussolini still wanted to pick the moment that was right for him, since he knew that Italy's weak military readiness only permitted a very short war. Low stakes had to capture high returns. The date for Italy's entry into war would be set, however, far less by the Duce than by the military successes scored by Germany. Hence, on May 10, during the unspeakable German aggression against Belgium, the Netherlands, and Luxembourg, there were grounds to fear for a moment that Mussolini would get carried away into striking a "heroic" and gainful posture. But he decided to wait a while longer and see how things turned out. Sir Percy Loraine and François-Poncet called on Ciano to sound him out. He assured them that Italy's stance would remain the same, for there was no reason why it should adopt a different attitude toward the attack on Belgium, the Netherlands, and Luxembourg than it had kept during the invasion of Denmark and Norway. He added that this stance of nonbelligerence agreed in all points with the commitments made to Germany by Italy; he further implied that this stance would not last forever. The British ambassador, in whose house I was having lunch on that fateful May 10, confided to me that Ciano had even said to him: "The answer I am giving you is not a pledge for the future. Our state of nonbelligerence could last a month [and it did] or two months, or two years, for it depends solely on the general situation. The Duce keeps all his options open. In any case, you will be forewarned in time." Sir Percy Loraine smiled wryly: "What do you mean by that? Twenty-four hours of advance notice?" Now Ciano smiled, "No, don't worry, you will be told reasonably ahead of time." These utterances offered Sir Percy a bit of relief, at least as to the degree of imminent danger. My French colleague perceived things differently. To him Fascist manifestos with headlines about "Britain's failure" and the nervous mood of the Palazzo Chigi looked like clear signs that the die had already been cast.

Buti, Palazzo Chigi's political director, tried in vain to hide his agitation under purported "peace assurances," which were nothing of the kind. He even told me that the virulently anti-French and anti-British rhetoric of the Fascist press did not necessarily reflect the government's opinion. And to raise my spirits, he said as we parted, "These events are excellent for you: the spotlights are no longer aimed on the Balkans." Anfuso spoke to me similarly, though more deftly.

Nevertheless, people in the street, Italians of all social classes, were appalled and angered by this repetition and worsening of the 1914 assault on Belgium. Thoughts also turned to the distress of Crown Princess Marie-José, who was Belgian by birth. Anxiety could be seen on all faces: no good would ever come from this heinous crime.

A luncheon gathering of all heads of Allied foreign missions brought us to the residence of our Greek colleague Ioannis Politis. We were all horror-stricken. Countess Kerchove was weeping: she had sons on the front line, near Namur. Princess Maria of Greece, who was also present at this luncheon, said to me, "We must pray as much as we can." Lady Charles disclosed to me that Labouchère, a member of the British embassy staff, was struck for having ripped down an anti-British poster on the wall of the Regina-Carlton Hotel, to which he was going. From there he telephoned Sir Noel Charles, asking for help. Sir Noel came at once, but because he was in a dinner jacket and spoke English, he too was jostled and shoved by Fascists, who wanted moreover to haul him to their party headquarters. He in turn telephoned Ciano, who sent police officers to the rescue. As he left the hotel, he found anti-British posters stuck on the windows of his own car. He demanded that the police remove them, then he drove off with Labouchère.

Phillips told me that on behalf of President Roosevelt he had sent Mussolini a "very serious and solemn appeal," aimed at convincing him to stay out of the conflict—but meanwhile the Hungarians, doubtless egged on by the Italians, were threatening the Slovaks and massing troops. Mussolini replied to Phillips that he could undertake no such commitment, since he was bound to Germany by a treaty of alliance.

King Alfonso XIII told me during a private dinner that a reliable source had informed him that the starting date for the Italian offensive had been set for early June. He already knew the main points of the Italian-German agreement in the case of total victory by the Axis: Germany would claim a protectorate over all of Northern Europe's Germanic countries and would retake her African colonies, enlarged at the expense of the French empire; Italy, for its part, would see its boldest dreams achieved in seizing Savoy, Nice, Corsica, Malta, Tunisia, Egypt, Sudan, and Djibouti. It all sounded like the wildest fantasy. Anfuso, while not raving quite that far, nevertheless imparted to me his conviction that "the game is up, the Allies cannot escape their final defeat, victory is at hand, and the Führer's genius in matters of strategy exceeds human understanding." He pitied France, "which is about to pay a very high price for its political mistakes, induced by the petty mind and narrow outlooks of Léger" (secretary-general of the Quai d'Orsay). He led me to understand that very soon Italy would be in a position "to settle its old legal scores with France."

Now sold on the idea of a stunning German victory, Ciano himself was to announce to me the impending onset of Italy's offensive against France, already down on the mat. He called me in on May 31 to tell me that "Italy would very soon [that is, in the first half of June] take the gravest decision" and that its operations would be directed not east but west—so as not to draw the war zone into the Balkans. He assured me that Hungarian and Russian troop concentrations were by no means directed against my country. Italy and Germany could guarantee that, for "they would always keep a free hand." In a quite honorable way, incidentally, Ciano warned François-Poncet and Loraine that Italy would attack their countries shortly. He vouched that he would take care of their departure and would see them once again in the meantime.

A WAR OF TWO WEEKS

On June 10, 1940, at 4:30 P.M., Ciano summoned the French and British ambassadors in order to deliver Italy's declaration of war. Here is how he recounted these meetings in his journal: "I first called in François-Poncet, who was trying to hide his emotions. I told him: 'You have probably understood why I summoned you.' He replied: 'Even though I'm not too bright, this time I figured it out.' But he smiled for only a second. After listening to the war declaration, he said: 'It's knifing a man already down on the ground. I nevertheless thank you for putting on velvet gloves.' He went on to say . . . that he could not bring himself to see me as his enemy, and that he would never look upon any Italian as his foe. In any case, since a European modus vivendi would eventually have to be re-established, he hoped that a chasm would not open between Italy and France that would later prove impossible to bridge. 'The Germans are harsh masters: you too will learn that.' I gave no reply; it did not seem to me the right time to hold a discussion. 'Don't get yourself killed,' he said at the end, alluding to my airman's uniform. Sir Percy Loraine was more laconic and aloof. He listened to my statement without turning a hair or blanching. He merely took note of the wording I had employed and asked whether it was to be considered a forewarning or the actual declaration of war. Once he heard my confirmation that it was truly the formal declaration, he took leave with dignity and courtesy. On the threshold, we shook hands cordially and long."

In my personal notes, I find under the same date the following passage: "Before leaving Italy, François-Poncet recounted to me his final meeting with Ciano. The mood was somber and Ciano seemed grieved. As he handed over the war declaration, he explained that Italy had certain commitments toward Germany that it had to uphold to the very end, through joint military, naval, and air operations with her ally. The war declaration was communicated to Sir Percy Loraine in precisely the same manner."

An hour and a half after these meetings, at six o'clock, the Duce showed himself at his famous Palazzo Venezia balcony and announced to the crowd Italy's entry into the war. He declared with bombast that neither Switzerland, nor Yugoslavia, nor Greece, nor Turkey, nor Egypt would ever be attacked by Italian military forces. He hurled all his thunderbolts at Britain and France, "plutocratic and sterile democracies," whom he blamed once more for their sanctions and other policies against "proletarian and prolific nations." Loud prearranged acclamations rose up from the Fascists, but his broader public showed only apathy, resignation, and skepticism. I called on François-Poncet and Loraine to bid them farewell. We talked about insidious parting shots and "stabbing one's neighbor in the back." The British ambassador did not relinquish for a second his calm, gentlemanly dignity. From Ancona he will sail to Portugal aboard the *Conte Rosso,* meeting in the opposite direction Bastianini, who will be returning from London; from there, each will journey home on his own country's ship. I also said good-bye to Sir Noel Charles. My entire family went to the Palazzo Farnese and bade farewell to the François-Poncet family. The ambassador's wife, with tears in her eyes, embraced my wife. The French embassy staff was to journey back via Switzerland, but its final destination was uncertain, since Paris was threatened by the German army.

The Belgian ambassador, Count Kerchove, was enjoined by the Palazzo Chigi to choose sides between Leopold III and the Pierlot government, which had taken refuge in France. His reply was that he remained faithful to his king; at the same time, since the king had not appointed a new government in Brussels, it was evident that the Pierlot cabinet continued to be legally in power. Thereupon Kerchove was requested to leave Italy with the other Allied diplomats.

We also bade sad good-byes to the Hubrechts, the Dutch envoy and his wife, who were neighbors of ours on the Janiculum and very dear friends.

If the diplomatic clan was thus losing many members, it was on the other hand gaining an ambassador: Gorelkin of the USSR. Wishing to lessen the contrast between Italian-Russian and German-Russian relations, especially in the midst of war, Mussolini was trying to mend his fences with the USSR. It would enable him, he thought, to keep a closer eye on the relations between Moscow and Berlin. It would also preserve a direct contact with the only major power (aside from Germany and Italy) that would remain upright on the European chessboard following a possible European collapse and total German victory, and that might therefore help to prevent the Nazis from achieving 100 percent domination.

Their possible subservience to an unbridled and uncontrolled Hitler-led Germany: that was the scenario that Italians feared, even if they did not fear the likely results of their own "occupation campaign" and cravings for French territories. Hence their lack of enthusiasm, their pessimism, their surreptitious hope that, in spite of its defeat, France would not be completely incapacitated. Ah, if only one could have won a share of the spoils without going to war so soon!

On June 13, I sent our Ministry the following report concerning Italy's entry into the war: "The first days of Italy's war went by relatively calmly, without commotions that would have disturbed the appearance of normality. Until now, no strong reactions are to be noted in public opinion, neither hostility toward the countries labeled by Mussolini as Italy's enemies nor enthusiasm for the war that is beginning and in which quick victory has been promised. A total resignation and an unconcealed sadness, that is what can be read on the faces of most of the population. Anyone who has witnessed the first days of war in a country setting out to conquer long craved-for territories cannot but be astonished by the lack of exhilaration in Italy. One does not see masses of youths demonstrating noisily in the streets or singing patriotic songs, one does not see military trains with warlike or humorous inscriptions written on the carriages, one does not see, finally, troops marching through city streets, covered with flowers offered by the population. . . . The people are told that victory will be obtained at little cost and swiftly—at most in three months' time!—after which the wildest aspirations would be fulfilled: from Djibouti to Corsica, and from Nice to Tunis! . . . But so far, the anticipated early successes (as would have been the occupation of Malta and Corsica, or a landing in Tunis), which had been expected virtually to coincide with the declaration of war, seem to be delayed. The communiqué at the end of the first day of fighting was a disappointment because it only mentioned the bombing of Malta. And people in the know, or who listen to foreign broadcasts, have also learned of the Allies' accomplishments (the bombing of Libya, of Italian East Africa, of Genoa, of Turin), unexpected feats from adversaries deemed lacking in military initiative.

"Public opinion is being told that the purpose of this war—which is decidedly unpopular, especially in regard to the fight against France—is a unique opportunity for the fulfillment of Italy's aspirations. Since the Allies are doomed to utter collapse, Italy has the duty to seize its part of the inheritance that otherwise would fall into Germany's hands. Because Fascist prestige refuses to receive territories at the peace conference 'by the grace of the Reich,' the only acceptable solution is the occupation of those territories by the nation's forces. Thus presented as an occupying operation, rather than as the last blow given to nations struggling for their lives (which would not have been accepted by the sensitivity of such an old, refined, and so humane a civilization as the Italian one), the war is seen and accepted by the mass of the people as a sad but unavoidable necessity. . . . The people are nevertheless worried about the rebuilding of tomorrow's Europe on the ruins of today's. And this uncertainty is also felt by the leaders. A tête-à-tête with the powerful Reich appeals to no one.

"That is why the forming of a counterweight that would put the conversations between Rome and Berlin on an equal footing is seen as necessary. This counterweight, in the minds of the Italian political leaders, might be constituted by a grouping of Latin Mediterranean countries under Italian aegis, with possible supports in Central and Eastern Europe."

✧ ✧ ✧

During the early hours of June 14, from 1:30 to 3:30 A.M., French war planes flew over Rome for the first time and dropped leaflets. The Italian antiaircraft batteries responded in violent, deafening, and exaggerated fashion. We heard the crackling of flak over the San Pancrazio Gate on the Janiculum, a few steps away from our legation. What a pyrotechnical display in the beautiful, warm Roman night! As soon as things calmed down, endless shouts and exclamations were heard from doorsteps in the Trastevere. The next morning we, too, picked up some of those leaflets dropped by French airmen. Their tenor was: "The Duce has chosen to go to war, so here it is! Yet France does not wage war against the Italian people. Stay put! France will stay put, too!" Two nights later, and on those that followed, the same happened again. Since we could not sleep at night, a little rest was in order. Prince and Princess Rofredo Caetani di Bassiano offered it to us for a few hours in their charming country house in Ninfa, an abandoned and deserted city, like Pompeii, which seemed brought back to life by the charm and grace of our hosts.

Anfuso, replacing Ciano, who had gone for a few days to the "war front," told me that France, through Spanish channels, was suing for peace. "France is finished," he exclaimed; "If it had resigned itself to accepting a separate peace before the battle of the Somme, it might perhaps still have saved something. Now, however, it will lose its entire colonial empire, as did Germany when it was vanquished. If Britain gives up now, we will offer it gentler conditions, but if it prefers to wait until the final blow, it will share France's fate." I pointed out to Anfuso the risks of a "vengeful peace." He lifted his eyes toward the sky: "With geniuses like Hitler and Mussolini in charge, there is no need to fear any excess, for they will know how to restore balance and measure." Mackensen was to use the very same terms in a conversation I had with him upon his return from Munich, where he had attended the Hitler-Mussolini meeting.

We learned at that time that French Prime Minister Paul Reynaud had been replaced by Field Marshal Pétain, who requested from Bordeaux, and through the intermediary of Spain, a cease-fire. The wrenching felt by the old field marshal, the heroic victor of Verdun, was clearly apparent from the text of his message to the French people.

Now came the sad days of the Armistice, with brief negotiations in Villa Madama and Villa Incisa. The courtesy of the Italians contrasted with the brutal arrogance of the Germans in the train carriage of Rethondes. All the same, they hastened to seize the Villa Medici, the traditional quarters of France's academy in Rome, and that sickened Phillips, who was charged with defending Allied interests in Italy since the break in relations.

THE SOVIET ULTIMATUM TO ROMANIA AND THE LOSS OF BESSARABIA AND NORTHERN BUKOVINA

June 27. The tragedy of the Romanian nation was beginning. Early in the morning I received a phone call from Gigurtu, the pro-German businessman who that month had replaced Gafencu as foreign minister. He was having a coded message sent to me with the news that the Soviet Union had delivered the previous day—through a note handed by Molotov to Davidescu at 10 P.M.—an ultimatum demanding the surrender of Bessarabia and northern Bukovina. The reply had to be given within twenty-four hours. I was instructed to ask for the Italian government's view of our decision to defend ourselves. I was also to ask whether the Italian government intended to make representations in Budapest and Sofia to prevent them from attacking us.

I immediately asked to be received by Mussolini and by Ciano. But I was told that Mussolini was away from Rome for a few days and that Ciano would return from Leghorn only the next day. So as not to lose time, I went to the Palazzo Chigi and made my démarche to Anfuso. I phoned the following report to Bucharest: "Anfuso told me the Italian government had been informed of the situation by Italy's envoy to Bucharest. He read to me both Ghigi's cable on his audience with the king and the following instructions which had been sent to him: 'Italy's envoy will convey to the king and to the Romanian government that the Italian government considers it to be of crucial European interest—not only for Romania but also for the other countries—that Romania avoid a conflict with the Soviet Union.' As for possible démarches in Budapest and Sofia, Anfuso told me he had no instructions, but that I will be able to ask Ciano directly. Personally, he seemed certain that those démarches will be made, since they would also be in Italy's interest.

"I asked him how he saw the possibility of avoiding a conflict, since we were being asked to cede by tonight a large portion of our territory. He replied that we could propose negotiations. I asked him to tell me whether the Italian government was insisting in that sense in Moscow. He apologized, saying he did not have the authority to give me that information, but that he could assure me that, in agreement with Germany, Italy would do anything it could to help us, repeating that it was also in Italy's interest.

"During the conversation, he let it slip that the Italian government had known for three days of the Soviet government's intention to open the Bessarabian issue. I then asked why the Romanian government had not been informed immediately. . . . He answered that the Russian intentions had not become well known in Berlin and Rome until the last moment, and that it had not been known for certain that they would take the form of an ultimatum."

June 28. I began this tragic day by going to see Ciano. He seemed very embarrassed and smiled without purpose. I sent to Bucharest the following cable about this disheartening meeting: "I reminded Ciano of our past conversations, of his advice to resist the Soviets, of his pledges of military assistance. He admitted that what I was telling him was true, but at that time Italy was not at war. But now all of Italy's efforts and energy are devoted to the war against Britain, and Italy can have no other preoccupation. That is why he advises us to negotiate with the Soviet Union, since the inequality of forces is too great and no one will leap to our assistance.

"I asked him whether there still was time to negotiate and, if so, whether the Italian government would support us by advising moderation to Moscow. He answered in the affirmative, assuring me that this very morning he would speak to the same effect to the Soviet ambassador.

"I similarly asked him whether the Italian government would bring to bear its influence in Budapest and Sofia in order to prevent an aggression against us. He assured me he was doing the best he could to calm down the Hungarians and Bulgarians, and to prevent renewed turmoil in the Balkans. He believes he will succeed. He rules out the possibility of a Russian-Hungarian-Bulgarian agreement against us.

"I explained that we were asked to make a double grievous sacrifice: the surrender of purely Romanian districts that are part of our most sacred national and spiritual heritage, and the acceptance of this outrage without at least defending ourselves arms in hand. If we were to follow Italy's advice and resign ourselves to the inevitable, could we at least count in the future on deepened friendship from Italy?

"The minister of foreign affairs stated that Italy would take into account our sacrifice for peace in Southeastern Europe, a service we would render to both Italy and Germany. The convergence of our interests is total. He prefers not to talk of plans for the future. I got the impression that, at bottom, he was very depressed and that he saw the Bolshevik advance as a blow to the Axis, although he did not tell me so openly. I expounded all our historic and ethnic arguments, and left with him ethnographic maps. He seemed convinced, but kept repeating: 'A nation of twenty million cannot fight alone against one of one hundred seventy million, and no one will ever be able to blame you for not having fought against such a giant, running the risk of the occupation of your capital, if not of your entire country.' He spoke to me with great warmth, asking me to come whenever I wanted to see him."

As I was leaving, Ciano told me, while shaking my hand, that circumstances might arise that would allow us to right the wrongs imposed on us now, for no one can foresee the future.

Deeply disturbed, I then went to see Mackensen, reminding him that if we did not have better relations with the Russians, it was in good part because Hitler was telling us that the only condition for achieving good relations between Romania and Germany was that we do not improve our relations with Russia. This is the text of my ensuing cable to the Foreign Ministry: "I had a long meeting with Mackensen. With the help of ethnographic maps and statistics, I set forth to him our rights over Bessarabia and northern Bukovina, integral parts of Moldavia. He seemed convinced of the rightfulness of our cause, but asserted that at this time the last word did not belong to justice, but to Realpolitik. From the point of view of German interests, it is immaterial whether Bessarabia belongs to Romania or the Soviet Union. I asked him whether it was immaterial that Bolshevism advanced in Europe and took up new positions against Germany. He remarked it was only a matter of kilometers, and that a difference of a few tens of kilometers are not of major import to the Reich. He admitted, however, that it would be another matter if Russia tried to cross the Prut River. Germany would not tolerate that the Soviets encroach on Romania's core, with which it has such close and important economic relations. . . .

"Germany's ambassador believes there is no longer enough time to negotiate with Moscow, and that a rational assessment would reject a futile resistance.

"I asked him whether he did not think that the lack of resistance might be interpreted as a tacit agreement that would be used as an objection against us were we to raise anew the question of Bessarabia in some future circumstances. He replied categorically: 'If circumstances were to arise favorable to your taking Bessarabia back, you will take advantage of them and I can assure you that nothing will prevent you from doing so under the pretext that you willingly agreed to the surrender of that territory. Everybody knows that you yielded in face of an overwhelming force, and only to prevent pointless massacres and destruction.'

"I asked whether the German government would still be able to urge moderation on Moscow. He explained that that was out of the question and that Moscow would not reverse any of its decisions.

"I then broached the question of Hungary and Bulgaria's attitude. Mackensen is convinced they have no agreement with Moscow and that they will not budge. He added: 'In Moscow, we do not have the possibility of changing things, but in Budapest and Sofia we have sufficient influence to make them behave.' I drew his attention to Budapest's impudent tone toward Romania. He answered, 'The louder they yell, the more they prove they are unable to do anything else.' At that point we were interrupted, Mackensen being called to the phone by the Italian minister of foreign affairs. When he returned, he told me, 'Ciano phoned me to confirm his conviction that the Hungarians and Bulgarians will not budge.'

"As we parted, Mackensen showed real sorrow for the grievous days Romania was going through."

We were thus abandoned by everyone. Moscow, it was now known, had already informed Berlin and Rome of its intention to take possession by force of Bessarabia and northern Bukovina on June 24—three days before the presentation of the ultimatum. What was especially revolting was that neither the German nor the Italian government had found it fit to forewarn the Romanian government, thus becoming accessories to the crime.

As was to be expected, the Soviets refused to negotiate, and they demanded that the territories in question be evacuated within four days. Bucharest asked for an extension of the deadline, but Molotov granted only a few more hours.

On June 29, at 2:00 A.M., Soviet armed forces crossed the border all along its length, and by 2:00 P.M. Chişinău, Cetatea-Albă, and Cernăuţi had been occupied. I must record, with deep sorrow, that the Jewish population of these cities, who had always enjoyed decent treatment under Romanian rule, had the dastardliness of stoning our retreating soldiers in their joy at the arrival of the Communist authorities, who had many Jews in their ranks.

✧ ✧ ✧

July 3. A particularly distressing day for us; it marked the completion of the loss of Bessarabia, northern Bukovina, and of the district of Herţa (the latter especially sad for me, for it contains our ancestral estate of Bossia, near Şendriceni). I had the legation's flag flown at half-mast, and my staff and I went into mourning. I was then received by Ciano, and reported as follows my meeting to Constantin Argetoianu, our new minister of foreign affairs: "Ciano expressed his satisfaction at the Romanian government's decision to renounce the Franco-British guarantee of April 13, 1939. The Italian press praises the new direction of Romania's foreign policy. Ciano told me that, following representations made by the Rome and Berlin governments, any Hungarian or Bulgarian aggression against Romania is out of the question. The grave incidents provoked by the Hungarians at the Romanian border have seriously displeased the Axis's two great powers, which have used all their authority in Budapest to calm spirits. Ciano added: 'The German government, in particular, took the matter very seriously and spoke in Budapest so explicitly and with so much force that I doubt there is a single Hungarian who would dare to take the responsibility of a reckless action. I believe they have finally understood there that if the Hungarian government were to provoke an armed conflict in the Balkans, they would act directly counter to the interests of Germany and Italy.' I had the impression that, this time, the Italian government had really been irritated by the Hungarians' attitude, about which they had never in the past spoken so bluntly. . . . The two governments are equally set against a Hungarian adventure. . . .

"The Soviet military authorities' interruption of navigation on the lower Danube has clearly upset the Italian minister of foreign affairs. He told me he would consult with the German government on this serious issue, which affects in the first place the Reich's interests. . . . Ciano repeated his wish to keep in touch with me during these days of crisis."

The resignation of the Tătărescu government was announced on July 4. It was replaced by a government headed by Ion Gigurtu and composed of the National Christians, the Iron Guard, and a few technicians, the whole being flanked by three generals. Mihail Manoilescu took over foreign affairs.

PRESSURE ON ROMANIA INCREASES

On July 6, Ciano was called to Germany, where he was to meet Hitler and Ribbentrop in Munich. After that, they were all to meet with Teleki and

Csáky, come to press their claims. Capece della Regina, former first secretary of the Italian legation in Bucharest and now attached to the office of the foreign minister, told me that, among other absurdities, the Hungarians are demanding the Szekler counties, with a corridor going through the heart of Transylvania. They were reportedly told to calm down as long as the offensive against Britain continued, and were promised subsequently a partial satisfaction of their claims. Teleki, however, was said to insist for one of the two following solutions: either the aforementioned corridor, or the partition of Transylvania on a southeast to northwest line, with the northern section to include the Szekler counties. Reporting the above to the Foreign Ministry, I added: "In case this information were to prove exact, I believe it would be necessary to put urgently at the disposal of the Axis governments all of the ethnographic and economic material that would convince them of the moral and material impossibility of such solutions."

As soon as Ciano came back I asked to see him. I reported to my government our conversation as follows: "I have just been received by Italy's minister of foreign affairs. I asked him if it was true that, at Munich, the Hungarian government had submitted a memorandum demanding almost the full reconstitution of St. Stephen's kingdom, and if the exuberant joy displayed in Budapest meant that some decisions had in fact been taken.

"Ciano began by asking me to recall the psychological makeups of Hungary's prime minister and of its minister of foreign affairs, both of whom I had had the opportunity of knowing for a long time in Budapest. Csáky, young, impassioned, craving success [Ciano actually used the term *bêtichon*[1]], and Teleki, older, more intelligent, more moderate, a geographer aware of what is feasible. And since it is Teleki who leads the government and since he is much superior intellectually to Csáky, it is he who has the last say on Hungary's demands. And these, in Ciano's opinion, are moderate.

"Hungary's memorandum will be studied in time, together with all the issues concerning Southeastern Europe. For the time being, Germany and Italy have in principle reached a decision, but are waiting for the appropriate time to actually examine the problem. We will be informed in time of the views of the Axis governments."

"Off the record, Ciano told me that in his opinion the best solution would be direct talks between Bucharest and Budapest, without dramatics or threats from either side, and only with the thought of establishing permanent peace.

---

[1]Featherbrained.

"I replied that I was personally convinced such contacts could be useful only if based on the principle of an exchange of populations, which alone would be able to eliminate the minority issues that have plagued Europe for two decades.

"Without answering directly, Ciano remarked that both we and the Hungarians would be called on to make sacrifices, we in regard to our present situation, the Hungarians in comparison to their pre–World War I situation or to their aspirations. However, the entire question is still untimely and cannot be settled in the present circumstances, and neither can it be settled through a reckless action by the Hungarians. Hitler told them flatly that he didn't want a war in the Balkans, and they got the point. Ciano repeated to me: 'The Hungarians will not budge.'

"I asked Ciano whether he was in a position to give me the same reassurances regarding the East. He replied that the situation there was totally different since 'we swim in mystery,' and that he had no direct information.

"Ciano confirmed that tomorrow he would leave again for Germany. He seemed disappointed by the way events unfolded. Churchill's speech last night burned the bridges and will prevent Hitler from making the peace proposals he had intended in his speech of the day after tomorrow. And the Turkish prime minister's address of two days ago had, likewise, a hostile tone toward Germany."

✧ ✧ ✧

At my return from a short stay with my family in southern Italy, I listened to Hitler's astounding radio address, in which he made overtures to both Britain and Russia, praising the latter for "not having overstepped its zone of interests." In the meantime, Italy followed closely, with anxious attention, the projects being drawn up in Germany regarding a future European order to be set up following a German military victory. Even though the alliance with Berlin should have guaranteed Rome a role in the fashioning of a new world system, Mussolini wanted to ensure that this role would not be in name only, as a figurehead. Efforts were consequently made to find out Hitler's real intentions and the actual consequences for Italy of the reforms planned in Berlin. No details were known, for instance, about the project Schacht was working on, which had as its objective to transform Europe into a vast political and economic entity, a sort of United States of Europe under German leadership. The idea, in itself, was not new. It was at the basis of the League of Nations, and was revived in Aristide Briand's plan for a European confederation, not to mention the *Paneuropa* of forerunner Richard Coudenhove-Kalergi. But according to what the correspondent of a semi-official German newspaper had told me in Budapest, Hitler, in his megalomania, foresaw the establishment of a Southeastern European system: on the pattern of the then British Empire, "the various small and middle-sized countries of the region would have the same relation with the Reich as the dominions have with Britain; each country would keep its head of state and the type of government it wanted, but in political and economic matters it would have to remain within the limits traced by Berlin."

The guiding principles of the scheme concocted by the Führer, so far as the Palazzo Chigi could find out, were specialization and decentralization. The agricultural countries of Central and Southeastern Europe would have to forgo their industrialization. On the other hand, the industrial countries would have to reduce the excessive protection given to their own agricultures. As for decentralization of the control and direction of economic life, two regional centers would be established: one in Berlin, the other—Italians hoped—in Rome. The first one would have in its purview the north and east, including Poland; the second, the south and southeast—that is, the Latin countries and the Balkans. Berlin, however, would have the overall direction. The Fascist leaders were transfixed by hope, but also by an understandable anxiety at the prospects that seemed to be taking shape.

✧ ✧ ✧

As requested by Ciano on July 23, I went to see him. He told me that Ghigi, Italy's envoy in Bucharest, had conveyed to him the Romanian government's proposal that Prime Minister Gigurtu and Foreign Minister Manoilescu, following their visit to Hitler in Salzburg, come to Rome in order to meet with Mussolini. Ciano told me the Italian government was in full agreement with the proposal, and only regretted that the present serious circumstances would prevent it from extending to its Romanian guests the official welcoming ceremonies with which they would have been met in other times.

✧ ✧ ✧

There occurred around this time an embarrassing, but rather droll, episode brought about by Petrescu-Comnen's unsated desire to play a policy role even from his relatively modest posting at the Vatican. He cabled Manoilescu that "a very important personality connected with the Italian government" had given him to understand that if Romania would completely align its policy with that of Mussolini, Italy would be willing to abandon its pro-Hungarian attitude and to guarantee the integrity of our borders. Shades of Alexandru Duiliu Zamfirescu! Manoilescu instructed me to check out this bizarre information. I asked Petrescu-Comnen for the name of this "important personality," so that I might confirm at Palazzo Chigi the authenticity of this sensational confidence. Clearly embarrassed at not having informed me beforehand, Petrescu-Comnen dillydallied in letting me have the name of his informant. However, faced with my insistence and my telling him I would have to reply to Bucharest that I was unable to check the story as long as I did not know who had spoken to our representative at the Vatican, Petrescu-Comnen finally revealed the identity of his alleged eminent personality: General Bodrero, long retired, who ten years earlier had been Italy's envoy to Belgrade. A most honorable person, no doubt, but completely out of the loop and with no links to government circles.

Taking advantage of my meeting with Ciano, and acting according to the specific instructions I had received, I asked him whether what had been told to Petrescu-Comnen tallied with the Italian government's views. Ciano answered me with a roar of laughter: "What idea possessed your colleague from the Vatican, and why doesn't he mind his own business?" All this prattle was just idle talk, he said, since he had charged no one to make such suggestions that flew in the face of Italy's unflinching alliance with Hungary. "In any case," he added, "had we had suggestions of any kind to make to the Romanian government, we would have made them directly, either through you here, or through Ghigi in Bucharest, but not through a diplomat accredited to the Vatican, and even less through an old retired general with whom I haven't met for years. Besides, it is out of place to think now of your role in the Europe of tomorrow, since the present stage of events does not allow the planning of the future roles to be filled by various countries." I was, obviously, duty-bound to convey this information to the Foreign Ministry and, in fairness, to the hapless Petrescu-Comnen.

✧ ✧ ✧

On July 26 I left for Brennero to meet the head of the Romanian government and his foreign minister, who were arriving from Salzburg. They acquainted me with the meetings they had with the Nazi leadership. Ribbentrop seemed to them very standoffish and pro-Hungarian. He found it appropriate to remind them of Romania's foreign policy during Titulescu's time. Nothing friendly or expansive in this man. On the other hand, Hitler, who received them for tea at the Berghof, seemed much more understanding and conciliatory. He seemed to detest the Hungarians and "that abominable Austro-Hungarian monarchy." If it hadn't been for "Titulescu, Gafencu, and the others," he declared, the German-Hungarian rapprochement would not have occurred. The Hungarians, he later added, are perpetually dissatisfied and complain continuously, even after the Belvedere arbitral award in which "they were given much too much of Slovakia." Nevertheless, Hitler stressed, Romania must reach an understanding with Hungary through direct negotiations, so as to calm things down. And the country that would break off those negotiations or that would start a war would be considered an "enemy of the Axis." The Romanian government could keep the German government informed of the progress of the negotiations, and the latter might eventually "put in a good word." Berlin, however, did not want to intervene directly. The Romanian ministers asked the Führer whether it would be possible, were an agreement reached with the Hungarians for an exchange of populations, for German troops to oversee the carrying out of the agreement. Hitler answered in the negative and suggested in exchange Italian or Spanish troops. Overall, Gigurtu and Manoilescu did not return with too pessimistic a view.

The next day, July 27, we arrived in Rome and were received at the railroad station by Ciano, other high officials, and an honor guard. We had barely arrived at the Grand Hotel where Gigurtu and Manoilescu were lodging, when all three of us had to leave for the Palazzo Chigi, where we held a meeting of an hour and a half, which Ghigi also attended.

The beginning of the talks was not very auspicious. Instead of trying to create a favorable atmosphere, Ciano took a bellicose attitude, trying to imitate his father-in-law, with glaring eyes and lower jaw thrust forward. *Commediante!* He brought up with no reason the sanctions imposed by the League of Nations on Italy during its aggression against Ethiopia, and then the Franco-British guarantees that were given to us. With a trenchant voice and pretended fury, he declared: "There are certain Romanians whose names are forever inscribed in the black book of Italy's history. I am talking of Titulescu, who dared call us savages.[2] I know one must not confuse him with Romania, but he nevertheless represented it when he said those things." As was only fair, Gigurtu reminded Ciano that Titulescu had never signed a treaty that could have dragged him into hostile actions against Germany or Italy. And Manoilescu added, "Without wanting to defend Titulescu—who nevertheless tried to soften the severity of the sanctions against Italy, at least in what concerns Romania—and who has now disappeared from our political life, I feel I ought to mention that policy is made by looking toward the future, and not toward the past."

Ciano calmed down suddenly and asked what we thought we might do to bury the hatchet with our neighbors for good. Gigurtu replied that his government was ready to begin at once negotiations on the basis of an exchange of populations, "since we don't want to turn over a single Romanian to Hungary." The Hungarian minority in Transylvania, he went on, could be consulted by a plebiscite as to their willingness to pass under Hungarian rule. If they voted affirmatively, one might cede to them an area of at most twelve thousand square kilometers, but in one of the richest agricultural regions.

Manoilescu then asked why the settlement of territorial disputes with neighboring countries was deemed so urgent. Ciano's answer was as follows: Romania, which gained so much as a consequence of the war of 1914–1918, must bring the disputes to an end, now that all the old settlements are coming under question and new borders are being drawn everywhere. Manoilescu then submitted many maps and statistics showing that the Romanian population was in fact spread beyond the borders drawn in 1918. He also asked whether, in the event an agreement was concluded with Hungary and that the agreement was later sabotaged by Budapest, Italy would take sides, or whether, like Germany, it would stay neutral. Ciano agreed with the German attitude, for to intervene or adjudicate was to make enemies of both parties. This had been the case in the Belvedere arbitration, where all the parties involved, including the Hungarians, had been dissatisfied.

Manoilescu then asked another question: in the event an agreement with Hungary was concluded, would his government be willing to undertake a temporary military occupation of the territory in question by Italian troops to oversee and safeguard the exchange of populations? For once, Ciano distanced himself from Berlin's views and showed himself favorable to sending an Italian police force to guarantee the execution of

[2]See p. 158.

the provisions of an eventual agreement. This was because, he underscored, "the Germans have only economic interests in the Balkans, whereas Italy also has political interests, being today a great Balkan power." Even though Italy did not want to intervene between Romania and Hungary, Ciano added, it could be kept abreast of the negotiations' progress, which would allow it to put in an occasional moderating word.

As had been the case in Germany, the meeting with the government's head was more cordial than that with the foreign minister. Manoilescu, at one point, told Mussolini, "If the Hungarians don't prove reasonable, we will come back to Rome." Laughing, Mussolini replied, "Do so, do so." The Duce complained somewhat of the Hungarians' endless demands. He acknowledged that a European order could not be established with huge Russia looming in the background, and that "this problem will have to be resolved."

That evening, I held a large dinner party at the legation. Everybody was enraptured by the splendid view of Rome that unfurled from the terrace where the dinner took place. Ciano was delighted by everything: by the panorama, by the table arrangements, by the caviar, and, since he was seated next to me, he whispered in my ear, "Wasn't I right in urging you to locate your legation in the Villa Ruspoli?" During our conversation, which turned toward politics, he proved, however, to be a false prophet, for he assured me the war would end in October with the destruction of Britain and of its empire. After dinner, Gigurtu and Manoilescu, accompanied by Ciano and me, went to the railway station for their return to Romania.

SEMI-OFFICIAL MISSION TO BUDAPEST

Called back to Bucharest by cable, to be "entrusted with a confidential mission to Budapest," I was received on August 5 by Foreign Minister Manoilescu. He told me that "the king, having a very high opinion of you, a view shared by the government," it was decided to entrust me with "a confidential and very delicate mission," that is, to make the first contacts with the Hungarian government in order to break the ice and initiate negotiations. My mission was to cover five points:

1. To let the Hungarian government know we wished to begin negotiations on all pending issues between our two countries.
2. To explain that the purpose of the negotiations was to establish a lasting peace between Romania and Hungary, later to be made part of a stable political system.

3. To urge that the negotiations start as soon as possible in the Old Kingdom,[3] at a site to be determined later.
4. To sound out the position that the Hungarian government intended to take about these negotiations.
5. To state categorically that the Romanian government would consider an eventual modification of the existing situation only on the basis of an exchange of populations, it being well understood that in no event would a single Romanian pass under Hungarian rule.

Manoilescu said I would be informed later of the date of my departure for Budapest, where, according to Crutzescu, Csáky had told him, "Bossy will be received by us most cordially and agreeably."

I took advantage of this respite to meet with my friend Grigore Gafencu, who had been appointed envoy to Moscow. He told me how relieved he was to have left the Ministry of Foreign Affairs, since the present circumstances made an unconditional solidarity of Romania with Germany inevitable, a policy that his convictions prevented him from carrying out. He heard that the Italians were accusing him of having accepted the Franco-British guarantees against the advice of Mussolini and Ciano. Gafencu was eager to make clear that he had met with the Duce and Ciano only a month after the Paris and London governments had extended those guarantees. He agreed with the idea of talks with Hungary, but only if based on an exchange of populations. He said he was happy not to have to conduct the negotiations, for which he felt that I, being respected and thought highly of in Budapest, was much more suitable. I replied that I would find nothing more painful and repugnant than to be charged with such negotiations, which should be led by a member of the current government. In Romania, the Liberals, the National Peasants, the Transylvanians with Maniu at their head, the youth, the press, public opinion, the armed forces, were all determinately opposed to a solution that might lead to a modification of our border with Hungary. All that was needed was for the king and the government to keep their resolve.

The next day, August 6, I was asked to leave for Budapest that very evening. I arrived in the Hungarian capital on August 7, where I was met at the station by my successor, George Crutzescu, with his collaborators and, to my horror, a crowd of Hungarian reporters and photographers come to see "the Romanian herald," and this despite the decision taken in

[3]Pre–World War I Romania, that is, excluding Transylvania.

common to treat my visit as entirely private and confidential. True, all the European press had drawn attention to my trip to Budapest and had commented on it. *Le Journal de Genève,* for instance, wrote: "Mr. Bossy, a former envoy of Romania to Budapest, will undoubtedly be welcomed as negotiator, since this diplomat, in spite of the difficulties of his position, has left in Hungary the memory of an upright and likable person." Similar comments were made by *Neue Zürcher Zeitung, Gazette de Lausanne, Curentul* (from its correspondent in Rome), *Giornale d'Italia, Corriere della Sera, Popolo di Roma, Tribuna, Il Tevere, Lavoro Fascista, Il Piccolo,* as well as by the Vatican's daily, *Osservatore Romano.*

Little wonder then that, after so much attention in the international press as well as in the Hungarian papers, the Budapest railway station was packed with people at my arrival, a fact for which I expressed my annoyed surprise to Count Julius Teleki, who had come to greet me in the name of the Hungarian government.

Passing first at the Royal Palace to sign Regent Horthy's register book, I went on to the Sándor Palace, the seat of the Presidency of the Council of Ministers, where I was immediately admitted to the room where Prime Minister Teleki and Foreign Minister Csáky were waiting for me. After the de rigueur exchange of pleasantries, I stated the purpose of my mission. I made it clear that this was only a first contact between our governments with a view to examining the possibility of an improvement in our relations. I added that, following the events that had shaken the very foundations of old Europe, my government was sincerely desirous of contributing to the peaceful reconstruction of Southeastern Europe and, for that reason, wished to settle outstanding disputes with neighboring countries. Keen, first of all, to establish solid and lasting friendly relations between our two countries, the Romanian government was willing to examine with the Hungarian government, if the Hungarians shared the same sentiments, all the outstanding issues between the two countries, with a view to bringing about a loyal collaboration between Romania and Hungary. After all, were we not the only non-Slavic people lost in a growing mass of Slavism? We were threatened by the same dangers, earlier for the ones, later for the others. If the Budapest government saw the situation as we did, I said in conclusion, I was authorized to invite it to send delegates to a site in the Old Kingdom in order to converse with our delegates about all the problems that kept the two countries apart.

In reply to my brief presentation, Teleki declared himself in agreement with the views of the Romanian government, whose sentiments regarding a future collaboration of our two countries he fully shared. He had, however, two suggestions to make, which I might convey to Bucharest. The first was that instead of a site in the Old Kingdom, he would prefer a city at the Romanian-Hungarian border, a solution that would make communications between the Hungarian delegation and its government easier. The second was that the talks start on Saturday, August 10. I answered that, with regard to the first point, I could assure Teleki that all the necessary measures would be taken to facilitate communications between the Hungarian delegation and Budapest, even if the talks took place in the Old Kingdom. As for the second point, the August 10 date seemed to me too close to allow even the technical preparations to be made for the meeting. Nevertheless, I promised to present his suggestions to my government. I then stated that since the Hungarian government had declared to me that it was willing to enter into talks with the Romanian government, I considered my semi-official mission to have come to an end.

My return to Bucharest was somewhat eventful. We left in a twin-engine Douglas, piloted by my cousin Constantin Cantacuzino, better known by his nickname "Bâzu." Everything went fine until Arad, where we made a refueling stop. But after Arad, one of the engines began leaking oil, and as we were turning around to return to the airport, so did the other. We had to make a forced landing in a field halfway between Lugoj and Timişoara, a landing that Bâzu executed perfectly. Informed of our mishap, the prefect put his car at my disposal, and I was driven to Timişoara, where I caught a train to Bucharest.

I therefore arrived in Bucharest on the morning of August 9, and was met by the minister's cabinet chiefs, who took me directly to the Foreign Ministry, where I was immediately received by Manoilescu, to whom I reported on my mission. I found him deeply embittered by the hostile attitude of Hitler, who, through his envoy in Bucharest, Fabritius, insisted that we make substantial territorial concessions to Hungary and Bulgaria. Accompanying Manoilescu, I went to Gigurtu, to whom I repeated my report, and then the three of us went to see the king. For the third time I repeated my report of the results of my mission to Budapest. If the Hungarians continue to maintain the same hostile tone as in a recent memorandum, Carol said, it would mean that they did not want talks. Speaking of the Bulgarian claims, he said we could not cede the Black Sea port of Balcic and Caliacra county, which are important strategically. Carol was visibly downcast and must have realized that his famous maxim "Not a single furrow" was an empty one and that his former bumptious position was crumbling. He gave the impression of a worn out, totally finished man. I had the presentiment that his reign was coming to an end. I never saw him after that.

Manoilescu thanked me warmly for the way I had carried out my mission. He seemed to be in a state of despair that fate had singled him out for the task of arguing about the country's borders with yesterday's adversaries. It grieved him that the fate of his beloved Balcic was now in question. He sent a memorandum to Berlin and Rome in an effort to save Silistra and Balcic. He asked me to go back to Rome at once to plead our cause. I wrote in my diary: "I leave the country brokenhearted because confidence in the present leadership has melted away and the monarchy's prestige is sinking from day to day. It is tragic to note that the difficult days we are going through do not find us united in spirit. Many old mistakes are now being paid for on the back of our poor country. P.P. Carp's famous apostrophe comes to mind: 'What a pity for this country, which was built by aristocrats, and has now fallen in the hands of riffraff.'

"The word riffraff is rather strong, but it is true that we no longer have the great figures of the past. Perhaps from within the ranks of our descendents great Romanians will arise, like those our nation has had at historical turning points and in times of adversity."

RETURN TO MY POST IN ROME

Returned to Rome on August 14, I was received that same day by Ciano. I urged him to back us up on the issue of the Quadrilateral and to help us save Silistra and Balcic, but he refused to commit himself, for the Duce and the Führer had decided not to intervene in our negotiations with our neighbors. Nevertheless, he added, he would seek an opportunity to counsel moderation to Sofia, because he believed the Bulgarians to be "reasonable men." But Ciano then launched into a violent attack against Greece, an active ally of Britain. I asked whether this could reach serious proportions. He did not exclude this, if Greece does not distance itself from Britain and does not make territorial concessions to Albania. Dark clouds seemed to be gathering over the relations between Rome and Athens. My Greek colleague, Politis, expected an Italian armed attack against his country quite soon.

In the meantime, direct negotiations between Romania and Hungary had begun in Turnul Severin. The Hungarians, giving proof that they had lost the last shred of common sense, were demanding two-thirds of Transylvania, with 4 million inhabitants, more than 2.2 million of whom were Romanian. After seeing Ciano at the Palazzo Chigi, I sent the following cable to my government: "I expressed bluntly to Ciano our surprise and indignation at the Hungarian demands, which can't even serve as a basis for serious talks. Our surprise is due to the fact that he himself had told me so many times that the Hungarian pretensions were as moderate as possible and that Teleki was the most open-minded Hungarian he had met. Our indignation is the more understandable since the Hungarians, who for twenty years have complained that one million of their nationals were under Romanian suzerainty, now propose a formula that would subject more than two million Romanians to Hungarian rule. I asked him whether, to permit itself such an arrogant attitude, the Budapest government might perhaps feel it would receive backing even beyond the bounds of reason.

"Ciano was careful not to express any opinion about the Hungarian proposal, for fear that if his statement reached Budapest it would be interpreted as disapproval by the Italian government. But from his ironic smiles as I described the solution proposed by the Hungarian delegation, I had the clear impression that he, too, found it excessive and frivolous. All he told me was: 'Your perturbation is understandable, but you must keep your cool. The Hungarian proposal is not in the nature of an ultimatum, but of a first negotiating position that can be argued about. We cannot intervene directly because, as I told you, the Duce and the Führer want to stay clear of these negotiations, but I will find out what the Germans' view is. Frankly, we have had no direct contact with the Hungarians in the last few days.'. . .

"I again stressed the wisdom and equity of the principle that territorial modifications should go hand-in-hand with an exchange of population. Ciano seemed to agree with our point of view. I wanted, however, to get an explicit reply, and I therefore asked him point blank whether he did not consider this principle to be just and logical. He hesitated a bit, as if weighing his words, and then he said, 'Of course it's logical, but we cannot intervene.' I replied that, even without intervening, one could counsel moderation and common sense. Ciano answered that he could not commit himself at present, but that he was following the situation and would consult with Berlin.

"As I was leaving, he invited me to come see him as often as I thought useful."

In the meantime, relations between Italy and Yugoslavia were souring. My colleague Cristić was worried by the presence of two million Italian soldiers at his country's borders with Italy and Albania. He did not exclude that, in the relatively near future, territorial questions relating to Yugoslavia might be raised. Allusions to an alleged Albanian irredentism in Kosovo were steadily increasing, he said. Yugoslavia, however, would never consent to such a cession and would prefer to fight, as it would also fight if asked to cede Macedonia in order to form a Greater Bulgaria. Small border rectifications in favor of Hungary and Bulgaria might eventually be envisaged, Cristić confided, as for instance the reestablishment of the 1914 borders. But the Sofia government was apparently very demanding, even having designs on Salonika, in the belief that Greece would lose this seaport and that Germany would not accept that it be annexed by Italy.

THE VIENNA DIKTAT AND THE NAZI-FASCIST DOUBLE CROSS

At 4:00 A.M. on August 27, the legation's first secretary, Metta, woke me up to read to me the text of a cable from the ministry that he had just finished decoding. Our government expressed its worry at the sudden recall of Fabritius to Salzburg and of Ghigi to Rome. It feared this might portend an Italian-German arbitration between Romania and Hungary regarding Transylvania, an arbitration we could not assent to without having first been able to present our case. I was asked so to inform the Italian government.

Ciano avoided seeing me, under the pretext that he had to leave immediately for Vienna, and asked me to see instead Anfuso, to whom I made the representation. Anfuso told me only that his boss was meeting Ribbentrop in Vienna "to examine the Romanian-Hungarian problem," and that no arbitration was contemplated for the time being. I pointed out that if the outcome were to be a so-called "friendly advice," like that of Hitler on July 31 regarding the Quadrilateral, it would still amount to a disguised arbitration, which my government could not assent to. As per the instructions I had received, I therefore asked him to convey to Ciano the Romanian government's insistent request that before the issuance of even a "friendly advice," a representative of Romania be heard in defense of his country's rights.

I had barely returned to the legation when Anfuso phoned with the result of my démarche: Manoilescu will be invited to Vienna, where he will be given the opportunity to present once more, and in detail, Romania's case. This promise proved to be as mendacious as the previous ones, since, as shown below, the Romanian foreign minister was neither consulted nor even heard. The next day, August 28, Manoilescu cabled me to join him in Vienna, where Ghigi, the Italian envoy to Bucharest, was also to be present.

I therefore arrived in Vienna on August 29, where several of my colleagues were already assembled: Alexandru Romalo, envoy to Berlin; Gheorghe Crutzescu, envoy to Budapest; Nicolae Lahovary, envoy to Bratislava; Mihail Pencovici, consul general in Vienna; as well as, from the Ministry's central office, Dinu Hiott, Blaga, Baltă, and Poloni. The Romanian delegation itself was composed of Manoilescu and Valer Pop, accompanied by Cornăţeanu, a former cabinet member; Sabin Manuilă, head of the Romanian Statistical and Ethnographic Office; General Dragalina; and Major Tilichi. On the German side, there were Ribbentrop, Mackensen, Fabritius, and Baldur von Schirach (Vienna's governor). As for the Italians, we found Ciano, Ghigi, and Talamo (envoy to Budapest).

After lunch, which we Romanians ate together at the Grand Hotel, Fabritius came to take Manoilescu to the Hotel Imperial, where Ribbentrop was staying. After an hour and a half of talks with the Reich's foreign minister, Manoilescu returned completely dejected, his face ashen and distorted.

He told us that Ribbentrop and Ciano had received him together. They warned him that there would be no negotiation, but rather (and contrary to all the solemn declarations made previously) an arbitration between Romania and Hungary. The Romanian government had to accept the arbitral sentence by 10:00 P.M. that very day, or else Romania would be attacked simultaneously by the Hungarians and the Russians, and "the Romanian state would disappear from the map." The two Axis foreign ministers added that this German and Italian arbitral sentence aimed at a synthesis of the ethnic principle and of the geographic situation, and that the territory Romania would have to surrender would be somewhere between 24 and 69 thousand square kilometers.

Manoilescu said he had protested vehemently, reminding Ribbentrop and Ciano that in Salzburg Gigurtu and he had been assured that any eventual surrender of territory by Romania would be based on the principle of an exchange of population, not on a "synthesis of the ethnic and geographic principles." Ribbentrop reportedly replied that the two Axis governments had become convinced that an exchange of population would not be feasible in Transylvania, and besides, "if the Saxons are willing to remain under foreign domination, other nations could do so as well." All of Manoilescu's pleas were apparently unavailing, and Ciano even told him that "a refusal by Romania would automatically place it among the Axis's enemies." During all the conversation, Ribbentrop and Ciano apparently behaved in a cold and brusque manner, verging at times on open hostility, and repeated continuously that "if the Romanians reject the arbitral sentence, their country will be abolished."

To somewhat justify their intransigence, Ribbentrop and Ciano claimed that Gafencu, our envoy in Moscow, had told his Yugoslav colleague that Romania's present policy was only make-believe and that as soon as Britain got the upper hand, Romania, as well as Yugoslavia, would help Russia against Germany. They added that Gafencu's appointment to Moscow had been a big mistake, but that it would be an even bigger one to recall him at this juncture. To soften a bit the cruelty of their decision, Ribbentrop and Ciano assured Manoilescu that as soon as Romania accepted the arbitral sentence, Germany and Italy would extend to it a solemn guarantee *erga omnes* of the integrity and inviolability of its territory. And Ribbentrop added, "We are not talking about a guarantee of the British type, but of an effective one: we would send you aircraft squadrons and army corps."

Bewildered and dazed, the hapless Manoilescu drew up a report of that rueful meeting, which was then coded and transmitted by phone to the government in Bucharest. It was 7:00 P.M., and the answer had to be given by 10:00 P.M.!

In his turn, Valer Pop asked to be received by the Axis ministers. He, too, he told us, pleaded for the principle of population exchange, but, of course, also without success. He, too, was promised a German and Italian guarantee if Romania accepted the arbitral sentence. If it did not, he, too, was told that we would be immediately attacked by the Hungarians and almost certainly by the Russians, Germany and Italy taking no further interest in the fate of the Romanian state, which would completely disappear. "You will have thus lost," Ribbentrop reportedly concluded, "not only the last shred of Transylvania but the very existence of your country."

Running into Ghigi, I told him plainly that we had been lied to twice: first when we had been assured by the Axis that the basis of territorial concessions by us would be an exchange of population, and the second time when we had been personally assured that the Romanian delegation was being asked to Vienna not for an arbitration but for an examination of the situation. The Axis governments were moreover treating Romania even worse than had the Soviet Union: the latter had given us twenty-four hours to accept its ultimatum; Berlin and Rome were giving us only three. Ghigi seemed highly embarrassed and confused, and tried to deny the reality. He reminded me that the Axis powers had always stated that they wanted to erase the entire ensemble of the peace treaties concluded in 1919. "Of all the provisions of those treaties," I asked, "including Trieste and Fiume?" "No," Ghigi replied, "because we Italians have switched in time to the side of the Germans." As for Mackensen, I did not succeed in getting hold of him. He most assuredly didn't wish to face me, after all the statements he had made to me that there would be no arbitration and that the concessions we might have to make would not take into account "the phantasmagorias of Csáky, that half-wit."

At 9:00 P.M., Bucharest let it be known that it was impossible to reply by the appointed time, since for a decision of such importance it was necessary to receive the approval not only of the Council of Ministers but also of the Crown Council, which would be able to meet only the next morning. A respite was granted, but only until midnight. Later, the respite was extended to 3:00 A.M. It was only at 3:40 A.M. that we received Bucharest's final answer: the Crown Council had accepted the arbitral sentence by nineteen votes to eleven. It was a staggering tragedy imposed on a country that had not been vanquished, and that was not even at war with anyone.

August 30. The blackest day—until then—in the history of the Romanians. Manoilescu and Pop were escorted by Fabritius to Belvedere Palace where, at 4:00 A.M., they were apprized of the arbitral sentence. The map containing the new delimitations was then placed in a sealed envelope that was to be taken by Romalo by plane to the king. I later badgered Fabritius to tell me which was the line that would split my country. Driven into a corner, he revealed to me that "You are losing the Szekler region. Unfortunately, you are also losing Cluj. But you are left with the guarantee of the two great powers, which should not be underestimated."

Returned to the hotel ashen-faced and teary-eyed, Manoilescu related to us the unfolding of the tragedy. Arrived in front of Ribbentrop and Ciano, he was told there was no need to plead his country's cause, since the situation was well known to the arbitrators. When Ribbentrop stood up to read the sentence (Ciano, Pop, Teleki, and Csáky being also present), Manoilescu asked for the floor. He was told he would be able to speak once the arbitral sentence had been read. As Manoilescu began to feel unwell, Ribbentrop interrupted his reading and requested that a glass of water be given to the Romanian foreign minister. When he was shown the map with the new demarcation, Manoilescu reeled, close to collapse. When he recovered, he again requested leave to speak. He was told that the acceptance of the arbitral sentence had to be signed first, and that it was only after that that statements could be made. Flustered, the hapless Manoilescu signed, but he was again swindled by the two arbitrators, who, contrary to their earlier promises, said that now that the deed had been done, statements by the parties involved had become of no use. At that point Manoilescu fainted and had to be carried into an adjoining room where he was stretched out on a couch and given an injection to bring him to.

This is how, through treachery, fraud, and surprise, Greater Romania was temporarily destroyed, first by Stalin, and then by Hitler and Mussolini through their stooges, Ribbentrop and Ciano. But history has brought a first healing of the wounds sustained by Romania. Transylvania in its entirety has returned to the fatherland, in anticipation of the day when the other regions torn away from the country will find their way back.

As for Nazi Germany and Fascist Italy, they met the fate they had prepared for Romania: Germany has lost forever its eastern territories, while Italy lost not only the countries whose independence it had recently snatched, such as Ethiopia and Albania, but also all its African possessions, as well as Fiume. As for the two executioners, who cynically and brutally carried out the orders to crush Romania, fate meted out to them the punishment they deserved: both were sentenced to death at the end of the war: Ciano was shot by a military execution squad in Verona, and Ribbentrop, as war criminal, was hanged in Nuremberg.

✧ ✧ ✧

The tragic events that sundered the country could not but be followed by deep internal upheavals. On September 5, a new political regime was installed in Romania. Carol was forced to yield most of his powers to the new prime minister, General Ion Antonescu, who became in effect the country's dictator. He was officially charged with "steering the Romanian state," while the king was to reign, but no longer to rule. The elimination of the "royal camarilla" began, the first victim being Urdăreanu, who was removed from his post at the Palace. All the following night, demonstrations demanding Carol's abdication took place in Bucharest. All the political parties—including, obviously, the Iron Guard—made this a precondition to their taking part in the next government. Then on September 6 General Antonescu sent a letter to the king asking him to abdicate, and stressing the gravity of the responsibility he would shoulder were he not to leave immediately. Finally, at daybreak Carol made up his mind to relinquish the throne in favor of his son, who, for the second time in his short life, was proclaimed Michael I, King of Romania. After that, General Antonescu addressed a warm appeal to the mother of the young monarch, Princess Helen, "whose sufferings are now coming to an end," asking her to return as soon as possible to Romania in order to stand beside her son. The Italian press, as one, hailed the new regime.

The Gigurtu government was acting as caretaker, and Manoilescu, still at the head of the Ministry of Foreign Affairs, phoned me in the morning of September 8. He informed me that the train in which former King Carol was traveling to Switzerland would be passing today through Italy, but since all the formalities had been fulfilled in Bucharest, I needn't do anything more. He added that the Swiss government had granted Carol asylum for only one month. The French government was asked if it would allow Carol to settle in France, but there had been no reply so far. The Spanish government was allowing only transit through its territory. The Portuguese government, alone, was prepared to grant Carol permanent residency, because his grandmother had been queen of Portugal, but even this under the express condition that the exiled king undertake no political activity.

Manoilescu asked me during the same phone call to accompany the now Queen Mother Helen when she returned to Romania. For the time being she was in Dresden, at the *Weisser Hirsch,* but she was due to arrive in Florence in the next few days.

On September 10, Urdăreanu called me from Lugano. On Carol's behalf, he asked me to have the Italian government authorize a new transit through its territory; owing to the collapse of a French bridge near the Swiss border, Carol could reach France only through Modena, Italy, in order to pursue his journey toward Portugal. I made the required démarche, the request was granted, and I called Lugano with that information. Carol thanked me and asked, "What news from Romania?" What news could I give him? That his railway car had been riddled with bullets when passing through Timişoara? He knew that better than I did! Besides, I had not received hard news from Bucharest, only the rumor of a true hecatomb among generals and "outsider" envoys (that is, political appointees, not promoted from the Ministry's staff), and the replacement of the chief justice and of the attorney general.

After the swearing of allegiance to Michael I by the entire staff of the legation, I went on September 11 to see Ciano, in order to keep him abreast of developments in Romania. I must admit that I had to force myself to set eyes upon one of the two butchers who had shattered my country's territory. But duty is duty! The Italian foreign minister assured me of the interest with which his government was following the current consolidation of the Romanian state under the leadership of General Antonescu—about whom neither he nor I at that time knew much. "Even though reduced in size," Ciano told me, "Romania is today more compact. The only issue that kept us apart until now was the commitment we had taken toward Hungary. That is why I always said that the road from Bucharest to Rome passed through Budapest. Now that we have paid our debt to the Hungarians and have obtained for them what we had promised, nothing remains, either directly or indirectly, in the way of a rapprochement between our two countries." I replied that the wound inflicted on us was too harrowing and recent for me to feel able to comment on what had happened. The only observation I allowed myself to make was that the Vienna award, far from consolidating peace in Southeastern Europe, would, on the contrary in my opinion, trigger fierce hatreds and unending turmoil.

In a report sent at that time to the Ministry, I wrote among other things: "All the governments, and especially those in Berlin and Rome, were perfectly well informed of the situation in Transylvania.... Besides, it was not argued in Vienna that we were losing such an extended part of Transylvania because it was ethnically Hungarian; it was stated that the arbitral sentence from Belvedere Palace was decided 'on the basis of urgent and weighty political reasons.' To sum up, we were stricken down not by ignorance of the ethnic situation in Transylvania but because political circumstances made it necessary not to take account of it. This interpretation, which was corroborated by the semi-official Italian periodical *Relazione Internationale* in its issue of September 7, allows us the hope that the time will come when the cited 'urgent political reasons' will no longer exist, and that it will be possible to return to the old principle of nationalities, which, despite recent assertions, has not brought only calamities to Europe."

It was very difficult in those days to ascertain the reason for which Hitler, who had so often stated he would not interfere in the settlement of the dispute between Romania and Hungary, suddenly decided to reverse course and impose an arbitral sentence that favored Hungary at

Romania's expense. In a report of September 19, I mentioned the hypothesis most credited in diplomatic circles. Here are some excerpts from that report: "The Soviet ultimatum on Bessarabia and northern Bukovina, as well as our acceptance of Moscow's demands, offered the Hungarian government the sought-after opportunity of adopting a more active stance. Knowing Germany's desire to avoid a conflagration in Southeastern Europe, the Budapest government openly played the Russian card. It explained that Hungarian public opinion would force its hand to attack Romania concomitantly with a new advance of the Red Army into the country and an attack by Bulgaria. Faced with this threat of an extension of the war toward the Balkans, the Axis governments changed their position and decided to give Hungary partial satisfaction even before a general peace. . . . Indeed, a new Russian threat was apparently looming at that time against our territory, its first objectives being Galaţi and Dobrudja, in order to establish a direct link with Bulgaria. The Hungarians were said to have stated flatly that they would join in by launching an attack against Romania. The incidents that took place on our eastern and western borders on the eve of the Vienna meeting might be interpreted as a sign of collusion between the Soviets and Hungary. Some go as far as to believe that a secret agreement was concluded between Moscow and Budapest during the visit of a Hungarian pseudo-economic delegation to the Soviet capital. Even if things did not go that far, it is likely that the Hungarians, aware of Russia's aggressive intentions toward Romania, availed themselves of the situation to blackmail Berlin by threatening an attack against us, which would inevitably have led to a wider conflagration and to the destruction of our oil fields.

"Germany had but two alternatives: either to make Hungary behave by force, if need be by a military occupation, or to give it sufficiently great gains to appease it, and perhaps even to win it over in the event of a conflict with Russia. The first alternative was a non-starter because of the close links between Italy and Hungary. There thus remained but the second alternative, that of a partial satisfaction of Hungary's claims so as to dissuade it from stirring. . . . As is often the case with blackmails, Hungary's blackmail succeeded. . . .

"With regard to the fixing of the demarcation line in Transylvania, the Italian former legation secretary in Bucharest, Marquess della Rosa, member of the commission charged by Ciano to propose a definite solution for the establishment of a new border between Romania and Hungary, disclosed to me that the line they had decided upon and that they had prepared for Ciano to propose to the German government left on our side the Szekler counties and Cluj. Della Rosa concluded that there must have arisen, in Obersalzberg and Vienna, a new and powerful reason for altering the line in so detrimental a way for Romania."

Ciano was to confirm indirectly della Rosa's statement when he told me, on the eve of my departure from Rome: "There were two proposals for the delimitation of your border: the one advanced by Germany, the other by Italy. All I can tell you is that the less unfavorable for you was the Italian one." I later found out that the German proposal had been imposed by the Reich's General Staff. It was known that Hungary was more closely bound to the Axis than Romania. By bringing Hungary closer to the Carpathians, the German army had the possibility of reaching at any time the crest of those mountains.

QUEEN MOTHER HELEN'S RETURN TO ROMANIA

As per the government's instructions, I drove to Florence on September 11, to invite the mother of our new king to return to Romania as "Queen Mother," and to accompany her to the Italian-Yugoslav border. I transcribe below the notes I made in my private diary: "Around 10:30 A.M. [on September 12] I arrived at the enchanting Villa Sparta, in San Domenico di Fiesole. I was immediately received by Queen Mother Helen, still good-looking and charming even though it is ten years since I last saw her. I told her: 'May it please Your Majesty to accept my respectful and heartiest wishes for the reign of King Michael, and may I express, Ma'am, the joy and happiness with which all Romanians greet the return to their country of the queen they have so long been deprived of.' She winced a bit at the expression 'Your Majesty.' 'Must you really call me that?' I replied that her official title was 'Her Majesty the Queen Mother of Romania.'

'But to be a queen, you have to be married to a king, and I cannot marry my son. You know very well that when Carol became a king, we were divorced.'

'The Romanians would be so happy if you allowed them to call you their queen. They miss a queen so badly. We all want to look up to you.'

'But can't you look up to me if I don't wear that title?'

'I think your authority and influence would be greater on the masses if you wore the title of queen mother.'

'Do you really think so? Well, then call me as you want! I am so sorry you took all that trouble to come from Rome just to see me.'

After asking about my family, the queen mother began talking of the situation in Romania, with a visible effort at objectivity. She told me that, in her opinion, it was a mistake to banish Carol in such difficult times, for 'he was clever and had experience, and I think he did his best.' She was terrified at the thought of the responsibilities that would weigh on her son's shoulders.

'He is just a child, you know, and he knows nothing. Not even foreign languages. He can't speak English properly, he speaks French à la 'vai Madam,'[4] as I call it, and his father never let him speak privately to anybody, not even to his ministers. He told me he had even to bribe the servants in order to get a newspaper, so they prevented him from getting any knowledge of what was going on.' I explained to her that it was precisely to complete his education that she was being called back.

'But it is too late now. When Mickey was a child and needed me badly, they drove me out. Now they call me back, when I can be of no use whatever. He is nineteen now. How can I make him do *dictées* with a French teacher: *'J'ai, tu as, il a,'* and so on? As for the political part, I will be no good as I don't want to meddle in politics.'

'You were very needed when your son was a child, but I am afraid your presence is just as necessary now to help the young king, who is quite alone, with not a single member of his family near him.'

'And then, how will I get on with my sister-in-law, Elizabeth, who is in Romania? You know, she slapped me once, the last time we met.' I made a gesture of incredulity. 'Yes, she did. She told me I had wanted to drive the family away during the Regency and had tried to suppress her mother's influence. And then she added, 'now, get this from me' and gave me such a hard blow in the face that I nearly fell down.'

Unbelievable! What manners! I expressed the opinion that the former Queen Elizabeth of Greece would try to draw closer to her, now that she had become the first lady in the land. Besides, even amputated, Romania was sufficiently large to make it possible to avoid overly frequent meetings. But with her inborn sense of dignity, the queen mother told me she didn't want to give the people the spectacle of family dissensions.

She then asked me to describe to her Romania's internal and external situations. She seemed moved when I recounted the tragedy through which the country had passed. She wants to lead as simple and unassuming a life as possible. She would like to make economies everywhere, and especially at the court. Given the ostentation of the preceding reign, she very adroitly wants to take the opposite course. She told me she would want as small a court as feasible: one marshal, perhaps two ladies-in-waiting, aides-de-

[4]Hodgepodge of Romanian and fractured French.

camp rotated every three months so that they not gain undue influence, and from the previous staff, only the aged Mocsonyi might be kept on. Nothing that would allow a new clique or camarilla to take root. She added: 'At my father's in Athens, we used to lead a very quiet and modest life. Our *train de maison*[5] was much below that of, let us say, a simple duke in England!' Then, looking almost with sorrow at her beautiful house, she said: 'I do hope Antonescu won't force me to give up this place and will let me come here sometimes. Anyhow, I will leave it to my son, and he may always want a rest up here. You see, these years have been dreadful for me, but still I can say I spent happy and quiet days here.'. . .

She found I was making too much 'fuss' about her return. I explained that we wanted her to see 'how sorry we feel for all that has happened.' Very *grande dame,* she replied: 'But the Romanians did no wrong to me. Not even Carol, he was quite decent to me. It is only the horrid Lupescu, who was jealous and tried to suppress me, even in the heart of my child. How could the Romanians stand her? Why did no Romanian tell Carol: we want to keep you as king, but throw that woman out! You know, she taught the child that, once he is married, he can still keep a lady-friend, because it is always done. She used to tell him, 'If ever you want anything from your father, ask it through me, as I make him do whatever I want.' She used always to come in his room, and when he was ill in bed, she sat on his bed. The child hated her. He never saw his father alone, and when he said anything, Carol used to tell him, 'Shut up.' Carol does not love his son. When my mother-in-law, whom I really was devoted to, told me once: 'Carol has many defects, but one quality: he loves his son,' I answered that Carol had lots of qualities, excepting one: he did not love his son.'

We kept talking for a long time, and she had me visit the entire house and its terraces. Nelly Catargi, once again lady-in-waiting, came to join us, and all three of us chatted like old friends.

In the afternoon, Nelly and I made a tour of Florence by car. She fears the influence of the German physician Warnekros over 'Sitta,' as the queen is called by her familiars. He has gotten into her head that she suffers from a nervous disorder and that she must not take upon herself the role of queen, lest she become completely exhausted. And because she is somewhat of a hypochondriac, she takes anything this doctor tells her as Gospel truth. It would make a very bad impression in Romania if she avoided the duties that are incumbent on her. I fully agree with Nelly.

---

[5]Style of living.

The next day, September 13, Queen Helen left for Romania, accompanied by me as far as the Yugoslav border. Her sister, Irina, Duchess of Spoleto, traveled with us up to Venice. At Venice, former Prince Nicholas came on board, and got off in Trieste. I invited the queen and Nelly to have lunch with me in the dining car, between Trieste and Postumia. Very relaxed and heart-to-heart conversation. The queen told us that Prince Nicholas seemed to be a sensible man and that he would be satisfied were his morganatic marriage recognized and were he allowed to settle again in Romania. He would even agree to come back without his wife during the first year. The queen told us of her son's innocent little flirts, and said how upset he was when he had to witness the violent quarrels between his father and the Lupescu woman. She believes it would be well if Michael did not delay marriage for too long. She is in favor of his marrying a girl from one of our great aristocratic families, a Cantacuzino, for instance. Were the Romanians to insist he marry a foreigner, one should choose between his cousin, Alexandra of Greece ("but she is not clever enough for somebody in that position") and Anastasia of Mecklemburg-Schwerin (who seems to be in love with him since she met him at the marriage of Crown Prince Paul of Greece, and who keeps his photograph on her desk).

We finally arrived in Postumia, where we were met by Cădere, our envoy in Belgrade, who was to replace me up to the Romanian border. As I was leaving, the queen told me: 'Thanks so much for your kindness, and I hope to see you soon.' Nelly whispered to me, 'She told me she found you very *sympathique*.' I answered: 'Well, it's entirely mutual.'

To sum up my impressions, I found Queen Helen to be very *grande dame* (which, unfortunately, cannot be said of all the princesses of reigning houses), for she spoke with so much dignity and generosity of her past sufferings and humiliations. But she seemed to me also to be very skeptical and disillusioned. She is persuaded that her former husband will try a second time to take the throne away from his son, and that everything will repeat itself from the beginning. She is also heavyhearted and scared at leaving her peaceful life on the enchanting Florentine hills for the political hornets' nest in Bucharest."

September 14. An Iron Guard state is promulgated in Romania. General Antonescu is proclaimed *Conducător al Statului*,[6] head of the Iron Guard regime, and prime minister; Horia Sima, commander of the Iron Guard movement and deputy prime minister; and Mihail R. "Lucă" Sturdza, minister of foreign affairs.

[6]Leader of the State.

September 17. The reunion of Sitta and Michael is said to have been moving, and the acclamations of the crowd delirious.

HUNGARIAN ATROCITIES IN TRANSYLVANIA

Meanwhile, the Hungarians had begun committing atrocities in the Romanian-inhabited areas of Transylvania acquired through the Ribbentrop-Ciano arbitral award. The entire male population of the village of Ip, for instance, was massacred, and photographs had been published of the pile of corpses. I felt duty-bound to send, on September 20, the following cable to Lucă Sturdza, the new foreign minister: "I believe it might be appropriate for me to remind Ciano of the declaration he and Ribbentrop made to the Romanian and Hungarian delegates after the Vienna award, that any infringement of the freedoms and rights of the Romanian nation in Hungary would be of direct concern to Italy and Germany. Such a démarche, made right now, would have the advantage that the two foreign ministers of the Axis find themselves together in Rome."

Sturdza's reply was: "I handed today to Germany and Italy's envoys letters in which, as per your advice, I officially and firmly protested the Hungarian excesses in Transylvania, mentioning in particular the cases of Trăsnea and Ip, where, according to the information we have, almost the entire male populations have been butchered."

With an inexplicable delay, I finally received the Ministry's authorization to lodge in my turn a protest with Palazzo Chigi, even though Sturdza's instructions were limited to the sentence "O.K., but in an entirely friendly manner." I was, however, firmly decided to express my full indignation at these crimes, tolerated by the Axis governments despite their solemn pledges. I went to see Ciano, but he was unavailable, being tied up with Ribbentrop. I then went to lodge my protest with the political director, Buti. I reminded him that the foreign ministers of the Axis had stated that the infringement of the liberties or rights of the Romanians in Hungary's territory would be of direct concern to Italy and Germany, and asked him to transmit to Ciano our appeal that he keep his word.

Finally, Ribbentrop's visit having come to an end, Ciano received me on September 24. I repeated to him the atrocities committed by the Hungarian population, police, and army against the Romanians in that part of Transylvania surrendered to Hungary. I pointed out the deep anguish provoked in Romania by such an inhumane treatment meted to our compatriots now included within the Hungarian borders, and which number more than 1,300,000. Ciano stated that he fully shared our sentiments and that, in accordance with my request transmitted to him by Anfuso, he had discussed this matter with Ribbentrop during his stay in Rome. Even though Ribbentrop said he had not yet been approached by us, he agreed for Rome and Berlin to send Budapest the severest of warnings. As for Italy, Ciano assured me he had spoken most harshly to Villani, Hungary's envoy (who was leaving the office just as I was entering it), declaring to him that the Axis powers were directly and personally responsible for the good treatment of the Romanian nationality in Hungary and that they would countenance no persecution of any kind. The Hungarian envoy implicitly admitted the crimes, since he ascribed them to extremist elements. Ciano told me he had replied that the Teleki government was sufficiently strong, especially after its recent gains, to be able to master the situation. Ciano said he added, word for word: "Teleki has sufficient armed forces and police in Transylvania to immediately arrest these extremists and throw them into jail; in any case, Italy and Germany have taken upon themselves the safety of the Romanians in Hungary, and intend to keep their word." Ciano had also cabled the Italian envoy in Budapest instructing him to speak very firmly to the Hungarian government on this matter, and authorized Italy's envoy in Bucharest to send, if needed, representatives to ascertain officially on the spot what had happened. Ciano stressed, however, the necessity of making the same representations in Berlin.

A mere four days later I had to return to Palazzo Chigi to draw attention to a new series of Hungarian atrocities in Transylvania. In the absence of Ciano, who was in Germany, I saw Anfuso and informed him of the latest developments, among others the hanging by the Hungarians of the priest, the teacher, the notary public and his son in front of the church in Tirimia. I pointed out that, in spite of the representations of the Axis governments, the Budapest government remained impassive in face of these savage persecutions, if, indeed, it didn't even encourage them covertly in order to exterminate the Romanian leadership stratum. Anfuso replied that the Fascist government was aware of the situation and that Italy's envoy in Bucharest was in contact with our leaders on this issue. Since after our meeting Anfuso was going to see Mussolini, he assured me that he would hand the Duce the memorandum I had prepared and faithfully report what I had told him.

When I spoke with Buti about these tragic events that resulted from an arbitral award that had not resolved the problem of the Hungarian minority but had opened the much bigger one of the Romanian minority in Hungary, he, not wanting to criticize his chief's work, preferred to criticize the Hungarian leaders instead. He told me that while Teleki was held in high esteem in Rome, Csáky by contrast had left a deplorable impression because of his chauvinism and lack of moderation and intelligence, and because his only object was personal aggrandizement in domestic politics. Similarly, there was profound displeasure at the obstinacy with which the Hungarian ruling class opposed social reforms, and in the first instance the redistribution of land from the great estates.

On October 8 I gave Ciano a memorandum of which I quote here the main passages: "The Royal government of Romania has proposed to the Hungarian government the constitution of mixed Romano-Hungarian commissions to investigate the innumerable massacres and atrocities committed against the Romanian population in Transylvania and to undertake surveillance in order to prevent future crimes and abuses in that region. The Royal Italian government has been informed of this proposal by the Romanian legation in Rome.

"The Royal government of Romania has just been informed that the Hungarian government has categorically rejected the proposal. . . .

"A new massacre of the Romanian population has taken place in the commune of Mureşeni, after the massacres of Trăsnea and Ip; this time it was not only the men but also the women and children who were killed. And this was not an isolated case. . . .

"Moreover, on October 5, 283 Romanian intellectuals—Msgr. Popovici, bishop of Oradea among them—were driven out of their homes with only three hours' notice, crowded in freight cars that were then sealed, and conveyed to the Romanian border at Curtici. . . .

"On October 6, three other freight cars filled with Romanians being expelled from Transylvania also arrived in Romania.

"At Cluj, three hundred families of Romanian intellectuals were driven from their houses on notices of only three hours, and shipped toward the Romanian border.

"Seventeen freight cars, packed with some seven hundred Romanian intellectuals, are at present in Löközhase, from where they are also to be sent to the Romanian border. The people locked up in these freight cars are in a pitiful condition.

"Such mass expulsions, worthy of bygone eras and in total contradiction to Hungary's solemn undertakings in Vienna, can no longer be tolerated by the Romanian government, who urgently requests the Italian one to intervene so that the Hungarian government return these Romanians to their homes and free them.

"The reign of terror continues. The atrocities perpetrated by the Hungarians in Transylvania exceed anything one might have feared. Hundreds of peasants, entire villages (including women and children) have been massacred in cold blood. The extermination of the Romanian population is proceeding according to a systematic plan that provides for the complete elimination of its leadership so as to stamp out the peasant masses more easily.

"The Romanian government has incontrovertibly learned that the Budapest government is firmly determined to accelerate this plan: persecutions, mass expulsions, executions. This is the fate that is awaiting a million-and-a-half Romanians cut off from their fatherland by the Vienna arbitrage sentence. . . .

"So far . . . Romania has reacted only through vigorous but temperate protests. The Hungarian minority in Romania, as the foreign diplomatic and consular authorities can ascertain, has no cause to complain. . . .

"The Romanian government insistently requests the Italian government to press Budapest to agree to its proposal for the establishment of mixed commissions."

Ciano appeared impressed by what I had to convey. He stated: "There is no doubt that the Hungarian government bears responsibilities in this matter. I constantly intervene to quiet down the Hungarians. This very morning I spoke in this sense to Bárczy, Hungarian undersecretary of state, who is presently in Rome. But what is absolutely necessary is for you to also keep the German government informed, because Ribbentrop seems to ignore the situation, as described to me, in occupied Transylvania. I had recently many opportunities of meeting with Ribbentrop, and each time I tried to talk to him about the situation of the Romanians in Hungary I found him uninformed, or only partially informed, on the issue. I have the impression that while you have come several times to draw my attention to these facts, no one from Romania has spoken to Ribbentrop about them. Given the complete solidarity of the Axis, I can act only together with the German government. Nevertheless, I will get in touch with Ribbentrop this very day to see what measures we can take together."

The next day I described to Mackensen the extent of Hungarian lawlessness in Transylvania. He replied that, "immediately after final victory over England," the Führer will establish lasting peace in Europe, and Germany will police the Danube Basin, preventing any excesses.

Once more, on October 17, I asked Ciano to press for the urgent and favorable resolution of our request that an Italo-German inquiry commission be established in occupied Transylvania, to which a Romanian observer would be attached. The establishment of a permanent Italo-German military control commission would also be useful. Ciano assured me that these proposals would be examined in the spirit of the new ties that are now beginning to bind our two countries together.

I was happy to see that my efforts seemed to be appreciated by my government. A coded circular memo of October 13 mentioned "Mr. Bossy has set up an excellent daily information service for Italian V.I.P.s, detailing all the Hungarian atrocities."

✧ ✧ ✧

Concomitantly, new incidents arose with Russia, which wanted to prevent us from navigating on the Chilia branch of the Danube delta.

I asked Anfuso on September 28 to describe to Mussolini the status of our negotiations with Moscow for the delimitation of the border between the two countries. Anfuso viewed the matter as very serious, given the clear efforts of the Soviets to cut us off from the sea, and he assured me that he would bring the Duce up to date. I also gave Buti a copy of my memorandum on this issue, for Ciano. Buti stressed that in any case Italy would never give up its role at the Danube's mouth and, in a related thought, he let out that even though the Tripartite Pact signed in Berlin had no anti-Russian tendency, it nevertheless took a stand against any possible intensification of imperialism by Moscow or the Third Internationale.

Talking with Mackensen a few days later about Russia's plan to appropriate the Danube's mouth, my German colleague assured me that, "after the end of the war with Britain," the Soviet Union would have to accept the Danubian role assigned to it by Germany: the Russians will not do what they want on the Danube, but only what they will be allowed to do.

According to the information that reached me, and which I passed on to the Romanian Foreign Ministry, the Germans were setting up a whole system of military defenses all along the European borders of Russia. The German troops that are crossing Finland toward Norway are said to be moving very slowly, and the presence of the Reich's forces on Finnish territory seems to become permanent, so as to be ready for any eventuality. The Ukrainian circles in Rome claim that German detachments are also to be found in Subcarpathian Russia, on the Soviet border, and that German officers have been seen on the streets of Uzhorod.

It was thus possible to perceive, and more and more clearly as time passed, Hitler's intention of undertaking a decisive military action against the Soviet Union at what he would feel the most appropriate time.

THE END OF MY MISSION TO ROME

The Iron Guard Minister of Foreign Affairs, Lucă Sturdza, informed me that, since Romania had declared itself an "Iron Guard state" in order to draw even closer to the Axis powers, it was logical that the posts of Romania's envoys to Berlin and Rome be entrusted to members of the Iron Guard. Consequently, Costi Grecianu was to be appointed to Berlin and Victor Vojen to Rome. As for me, I was to be transferred to either Vichy or Berne. Curiously, the news appeared in the Italian papers before I was informed of it! As a result of Dinu Hiott's insistent requests (backed by Manoilescu) that it be he who should go to Vichy, I was offered Berne. This, in fact, suited me better, both from a political viewpoint (for the Pétain regime, accused of collaborating with the enemy, would have left a rather unpleasant aftertaste to my mission), as well as from a personal one (our children were in school in Switzerland, and my wife and I had had since childhood close ties with this beautiful country). Besides, Lucă Sturdza's cable of September 27, in which he let me know of my transfer, was couched in the most warm and affectionate terms, and I answered him in similar fashion.

I then began making my farewell calls. First on Ciano, who warmly expressed his regrets at my departure, which he had learned from Ghigi, to whom, Ciano told me, Sturdza had praised me as being "one of our most capable diplomats, to whom an important mission will soon be entrusted." I then called on all members of the government and on all my foreign colleagues, who obligingly hosted luncheons and dinners in honor of my wife and me. Our friends Roffredo and Margaret Caetani di Bassiano hosted for us a luncheon in their marvelous Ninfa, after which we had tea in the ancient palace of the Enrico Barberinis in Palestrina.

In the meantime, Manoilescu arrived almost unannounced, wanting to meet with Mussolini and Ciano. He showered me with compliments: "You are the only true envoy we have. I wouldn't exchange you for the entire Ministry. I have been reading your reports as if they were the Gospel," and so forth. We went together to see Ciano, to whom Manoilescu also described the Hungarian atrocities. Ciano informed us of the setting up of the Italo-German investigation commission, which will include Roggieri and Altenburg. At one point, Manoilescu alluded to the grievous part he had

had to play in Vienna. Ciano reminded him that Cavour had had to sign the cession of Nice and Savoy to France. "Which did not prevent," he added, "another Italian from marching into Nice seventy years later." Did he really believe that Italy would annex Nice?

Shortly thereafter arrived my successor, Vojen—refined, likable, well bred. I wished him success in his mission, for which he confessed he felt insufficiently prepared. He was immediately received by Ciano, who apparently launched into a sharp criticism of Petrescu-Comnen. By contrast, Ciano praised me, saying I had been "the Romanian envoy I felt closest to." Very kind of Ciano, but even kinder of Vojen to repeat these compliments to me.

Before my farewell audience with King Victor Emmanuel III, Anfuso brought me the Grand Cross ribbon of the Corona d'Italia order, which the monarch had graciously bestowed on me. The king received me on October 22, as always unpretentious, full of wit and of personal charm. He talked to me of his recollections of Switzerland (because I was being transferred to Berne), of the war ("of which no one can foresee the end"), and of the caution Italy must exercise in its naval activity ("we have only five cruisers; we cannot put them at risk"). He also broached more sensitive issues: "If King Carol was guilty of only one-hundredth of what your newspapers accuse him of, it is obvious he had to go. He wanted, moreover, to be his own prime minister. Yet one cannot be at the same time king and prime minister. When one is a country's highest officer, one must not take responsibility for everything that is being done. Mistakes will inevitably occur and, since one cannot be everywhere and supervise everything, it is best to avoid taking responsibility."

He then recounted how, as a child, King Michael, being left once by his mother with the Italian royal family, cried when he had to leave Italy. "It is today the case of his envoy, Sire," said I. He laughed and patted me on the back. I thanked him for the kindness he showed me during my mission. "But I did not have the opportunity of doing anything for you," he replied. I reminded him that he had bestowed on me the Grand Cross of the order of Corona d'Italia. "That is true," said the king, shaking my hand lengthily and wishing me the best. I have kept a lasting and excellent recollection of this monarch, whom I would never see again, and whose life and reign came to an end in such sad circumstances.

Next day we left for Romania, before I was to assume my new posting in Berne. On the way, my family and I stopped in the places that were most dear to us: Assisi, Gubbio, Perugia, Arezzo, Florence, Venice. On October 28, we arrived in Bucharest.

11

Berne (1940–1941)

NOVEMBER 1940–FEBRUARY 1941

November 2, 1940. [In Bucharest,] I went to the Ministry and saw Lucă Sturdza. He reviled Carol for not having resisted the Russian ultimatum by force of arms. Once fighting had started, Germany would not have allowed us to be annihilated. Had the Iron Guard been in power, no one would have touched our borders. Nevertheless, he is absolutely convinced that in less than a year's time we will have regained our former borders.

November 4. De rigueur luncheon at the Swiss envoy's to Bucharest, René de Weck.

November 5. Audience with King Michael in Sinaia. Very likable and unassuming and, naturally, somewhat shy. He is very worried by what is happening in Greece. Being a nephew of Greece's King George II, he is anxious about the Italo-Greek conflict. I gave him a historical summary of the events that had led to the Vienna arbitration. He was wondering whether Germany and Italy, now that the investigation commission had informed them of the reality of the Hungarian atrocities, would take steps to bring them to an end.

Later that day, I had an audience with General Antonescu. He told me that since it had been decided to appoint Iron Guardists to Berlin, Rome, and Madrid, the government had had to find another posting for me.

November 7. After leaving yesterday morning from Bucharest, I arrived today Pallanza, where my wife and children were awaiting me.

November 9. After two wonderful days of relaxation on Lake Maggiore, with side trips to Stresa and the Borromean Islands, we all left this morning by car for the Switzerland we are so fond of, and which we entered at Brigue. Valais, the enchanting Lake Léman sparkling in the sun with a fragrance reminiscent of the Riviera, the Dent du Midi, all shielding this land of happiness and peace. We spend the night in Ouchy, at the Beau Rivage as usual.

November 14. Today, on my birthday, I presented my credentials as envoy of Romania to Switzerland. I am delighted. During my career, thrice have I asked to be appointed to Berne (as attaché in 1918, as counselor in 1930, and as minister plenipotentiary in 1935), but I never could obtain that posting, which I now receive without either asking for or expecting it.

Dr. Schlatter, deputy head of protocol, came to the legation to pick me up in the car of the president of the Confederation. In my suite were the senior members of my staff. The chancellor of the Confederation received us at the entrance of the Federal Palace and led us solemnly, in procession, to the president of the Confederation, Pilet-Golaz, who was assisted by Federal Counselor Etter. I handed Pilet-Golaz the royal letters for my accreditation and Gurănescu's recall. After the exchange of speeches, I introduced my staff. Then the three of us sat down: I in the middle, Pilet-Golaz to my right, Etter to my left. They began by extending their condolences for the recent horrible earthquake in Romania. Then, with more inquisitiveness than tact, the president asked me a series of questions: Does General Antonescu have the required political preparation? Will he be able to control the Iron Guard? Will the former king calm down, or will he want to recover the throne? Etc. Later, he confessed that the Swiss had their own difficulties, the main one being how to adapt to the new situation without sacrificing their traditions and freedoms. The return to the legation followed the same ritual. We all drank champagne. Let's hope this is a propitious hour and, God willing, not too short-lived.

November 15. Prince Nicholas, who has bought a villa in St. Moritz, came to see me. He railed against his brother, who had driven him out of the country. I reminded him that it was he who had brought Carol back, but he denied it, referring to letters—unseen by anybody—in which he advised his brother to remain in Paris. I didn't pursue the matter, but I had been at that time at the Regency and had seen with my own eyes how Nicholas was preparing Carol's return. Prince Nicholas complained about General Antonescu, who does not answer his letters and does not let him return to Romania. He complained in particular that he was no longer receiving the allowance he used to get from his brother. "From his own funds?" I asked. "As if Carol has ever paid for anything with his own money!" came the reply.

November 16. I began the long series of courtesy visits to the envoys of other countries. Today: the nuncio and the envoys of

Yugoslavia, Turkey, and Greece. They all believe the war will be a dragged-out affair, that "the game is not over yet," and that if it is difficult to defeat Germany, it is equally difficult to vanquish Britain. As for the Italo-Greek war, and despite the recent Greek counteroffensive, they believe that sheer numbers will carry the day. But they do not see what Italy's gain will be; what is of value is not continental Greece but the islands, which "Mussolini has presented to the British on a silver platter."

November 18. Today I saw, in turn, the envoys of Italy (Tamaro, my counterpart in Helsingfors), Germany (Köcher), Uruguay, and Belgium. Tamaro complained about the Swiss and the Federal Council, hostile to the Axis—with Celio, from Italian-speaking Ticino, the greatest anti-Fascist. Köcher had similar complaints. The persecution of the Mouvement National, the only Swiss party with sympathy for the Axis, was intolerable, he said. I asked him how come, then, does Berlin accept the Hungarian persecution of the Arrow Cross? "That is why," he replied, "our relations with Hungary are not one hundred percent cordial." But, he added, it is even more distressing when one is faced by incomprehension from blood brothers.

November 19. I saw, among others, Leland Harrison, the American envoy, and Kelly, the British envoy. They are both convinced that Germany will be defeated, overwhelmed by the aeronautical superiority of the Anglo-Americans. Molotov, they say, failed to reach an agreement with Hitler in Berlin, as proved by TASS's silence and by the coolness of the Soviet commissar for foreign affairs' cable to his German counterpart. Koch came to see me and informed me of the Mouvement National's dissolution.

November 22. Among the return visits I received today, the most interesting one was undoubtedly that of the German envoy. He virtually scoffed at the Italians. Whatever got into them to attack the Greeks if they were unprepared? A hope that the Greeks would comply with the ultimatum cannot substitute for preparedness. The Führer did not want a war in the Balkans. And mind you, added Köcher, if at least they had occupied the Greek islands, instead of offering them as a gift to Britain; Epirus, Thessaly, even Thrace are not very valuable strategically.

November 27. This is a black day. Massacres in Romania. The most notable victim: Iorga, the symbol of Romanian nationalism. If he was murdered by a Romanian, it is a blot on our nation's history.

November 28. I went to see de la Baume, the French ambassador, arrived from Madrid. He believes "Hitler is meeting with diplomatic setbacks," and the refusal of Spain, Russia, and Bulgaria to sign the Tripartite Pact[1] proves that "the game is not yet over."

December 19. Luncheon at the German envoy's. Recently returned from Berlin, he believes, as does his counselor Kordt, that the war will continue for a long time.

December 30. In a fireside chat, Roosevelt said today: "I do not believe the Axis will win the war." This conviction is obviously based on the best and most recent information.

December 31. Dinner and New Year's Eve celebration at the American envoy and Mrs. Harrison's. May God grant that 1941 proves better than the outgoing year.

January 1, 1941. Accompanied by my staff and in dress uniform, I extend my best wishes to the new president of the Confederation, Wetter. He believes the war will still last for a long time.

January 2–16. St. Moritz; the whole family. Perfect weather. At the Suvretta Hotel, one still gets the feeling of the old Europe of before World War I.

Prince Nicholas asked me twice to come see him, to request certain favors (gasoline, the sending of packages abroad, and so forth). He called his brother a "swindler." He was astonished that General Antonescu did not allow him to return to Romania, since, he asserted, "I would strengthen the dynasty." He complained that his requests for money were turned down unless he settled in Germany or Italy. But he doesn't want to do this after these countries—and especially Italy—amputated our country. He is convinced of the total victory of Britain and America.

January 22. Bad news from Romania. After being dismissed by Antonescu, Iron Guardist policemen [rebelled and] resisted in their station an attack, with tanks, by the army. The army is said to have withdrawn, but press agencies mention many dead Iron Guardists. On Radio Bucharest I hear Antonescu calling for a restoration of public order within twenty-four hours. On Radio Braşov—occupied by the extremists of Codreanu-*père,* among whom a number of Communists are said to have infiltrated—I heard a call by Iron Guardist workers and students asking for the removal of the "Jewified and Masonic" undersecretary of the Ministry of the Interior. What a tragedy has befallen us!

January 23. General Petrovicescu, who had been dismissed as minister of the interior following the assassination of a German officer, attacked

[1]Romania had signed on November 23, 1940.

the Presidency of the Council with six hundred extremist Iron Guardists (and reportedly a number of Communists). The army, firmly united behind General Antonescu, intervened and defeated the rebels. Antonescu cabled me that, with the help of the army, he had reestablished order in all of the country, and that "only from now on" will he be able to ensure a durable internal peace.

I passed on the news to the Federal Council, which, through Bonna, head of the Foreign Affairs Division of the Political Department, extended its congratulations, adding, "Any good news for Romania is also good news for Switzerland."

January 24. Details of the revolt reach us little by little. It was reportedly horrible. Heavy losses on both sides. Wanting to kill Antonescu, Petrovicescu attacked the Presidency of the Council with rifle and machine gun fire. The Iron Guardists in the government, with Horia Sima at their head, escaped to the side of the rebels. Antonescu ordered that Horia Sima be apprehended "dead or alive." The Germans seem to fully support Antonescu's reestablishment of order. The Swiss press is one hundred percent favorable to General Antonescu.

January 28. A new government has been sworn in, composed of generals and headed by Antonescu. It is a temporary stopgap, until calm has been fully reestablished.

In the afternoon, musical tea party at the ambassador of France and Countess de la Baume's. He told me openly that his former "and future" foreign minister, Laval, was *une abominable canaille*[2] who wants to get rid of Pétain and take alone the helm of the country in order to drag France into the war against Britain. If Germany wanted to impose the war against Britain on the field marshal, the latter would telephone Weygand in North Africa and tell him he was free to act as he deemed best. This would also be the case were the Axis to try to lay hands on France's African possessions. In such a case, Weygand would join forces with de Gaulle and Wavell, and Africa would be lost forever for the Axis. He spoke of the length of the war, of the "fantastic" American air force, and he even let out, "Mussolini is too intelligent to believe the Axis can still win the war."

January 29. Luncheon at the Chilean envoy's, also attended by Germany's envoy. The latter told me he was happy that order had been reestablished in Romania. He believes that, as in other similar movements, many Communists must have infiltrated the Iron Guard. This would be the explanation for the recent revolt. With regard to the war: "We say it

---

[2]A loathsome scoundrel.

openly, things are now going badly for us because of Italy's loss of face; this means we will have to do something." But he discounts the possibility of an attack in the Balkans or in North Africa, two areas in which the Reich has no interest in joining the fray. Italy's campaign against Greece "was an imbecility, but you too know the Italians!" We then spoke of Metaxas's death, which had occurred this morning. He deeply regretted it, since the Greek prime minister had succeeded in maintaining good relations with Berlin, even though they were fighting the Italians.

Sauerwein called on me. He said Pétain charged Laval with three things: that he wants to draw France into war with Britain, that he isn't truthful in his relations with the field marshal "and has gutter manners," and that he is dishonest (accepting bribes) and is planning to get rid of the field marshal.

February 12. Both the Belgians and the Dutch have recalled their envoys from Bucharest. Köcher and Tamaro believe that very soon Britain will, if not actually declare war on us, at least have the RAF bomb our oil fields. The Germans have thoroughly prepared their crossing of Bulgaria and will immediately attack Greece if either of two conditions exists:

1. Our oil fields are bombed.
2. Or sizable British detachments land in Salonika. The German government has officially notified Athens of the second point.

Ciano has informed Tamaro that the Bulgarians have agreed to the crossing of German troops through their land and that they will even adhere at that time to the Tripartite Pact, and that the Turkish government has stated to the German one that it would not oppose such a move and that it would react only were the Turkish border violated.

There were apparently some stormy moments in the last meeting between Hitler and Franco. Both Hitler and Mussolini cannot forgive Franco for his lack of solidarity in this war, despite old commitments and moral obligations. The purpose of today's meeting in Bordighera is said to be an effort by the Duce to paper things over.

[My brother-in-law] Ştefan [Cantacuzino] arrived on a mission. He tells me that in Bucharest one can see signposts erected by the Germans with the indication *Nach Pleven.*[3] There can no longer be any doubt.

February 19. Without prior consultation, my colleague Alexander Cretzianu, secretary-general of the Ministry of Foreign Affairs, informs

[3]To Pleven, a city in northern Bulgaria.

me by cable: "I have asked that you be accredited as the Romanian envoy to Berlin." Barely three months have elapsed since I took office as the Romanian envoy to Switzerland, and the current regime in Germany fills me with revulsion. Hence I try to turn down this new appointment, which my conscience tells me I could carry out only with the greatest reluctance. I sent Cretzianu a telegram to say that, while I am grateful for the government's trust in me and am eager to assist my country whenever I judge myself capable of doing so, I think that I cannot accept that post in light of my past activities as a diplomat, which were in the sphere of the Little Entente, the Balkan Entente, the alliance with France, and the British security pledge. In fact, it was on those grounds that I had been recalled from Rome three months earlier. If that factor was valid for Rome, it has to carry even more weight for Berlin.

Later that day, Cretzianu replied that General Antonescu had taken note of my observations but maintained his decision. And Cretzianu added: "Please accept my very affectionate congratulations for being named to our foreign service's most important post."

I grabbed the telephone to find an escape from this unacceptable option, but Cretzianu cautioned me that he will forward to Antonescu any letter or telegram that I send him on this matter. In a letter, he warned me that if I refused this posting, at a time when the government was struggling to put down the Iron Guard revolt, there would be heavy consequences for me. He appealed to my patriotism and spirit of self-sacrifice. In the end, I had to submit to destiny.

12

Berlin and Copenhagen (1941–1943)

I. 1941

PRELUDE

March 14. A gray, cold morning. I arrived with my wife in Berlin's Potsdamer train station and was greeted by an official from the Ministry of Foreign Affairs and my legation's staff. After that I took my first look around the rather dour, old-fashioned building on Rauchstrasse, in the Tiergarten neighborhood, which had housed our diplomatic mission for close to twenty years and which fairly soon would be reduced to a pile of rubble. I walked across its dark parlors furnished in a hodgepodge of styles. Fake Louis XVI furniture that would belong in a provincial grand hotel and that no one ever got around to discarding (me neither!) squats alongside the Far East—Chinese vases and rugs, Japanese embroidery and prints, and massive collections of jade. In the midst of all that clutter a few really good pieces, some even of museum quality. Why had all this stuff been deposited here? In months to come, colleagues from other countries would keep asking me about the posts I had held in the Far East (where in fact I never set foot), since they took it for granted that it was I who had imported into the *Diplomatenviertel* all that *famille verte* and *famille rose* porcelain, all those cloisonné enamels and Hokusai prints.

On March 18, I made my de rigueur call on the foreign minister to remit a copy of my credentials, as prescribed by García de la Vega. It is in the old-fashioned setting of Bismarck's chancellery that my official mission began. I walked in followed by a debonair giant, Baron Dörnberg, head of protocol. This career diplomat had spent several years at his country's legation in Bucharest, where he made quite a few friends and got nicknamed *Deutschland über alles,* on account of his six-foot-ten height. I was shown into the Iron Chancellor's famous office.

Before me stood a cold-mannered, stiff man, whose gestures were awkward and who tried hard to look imposing, but without much success. His smile, meant to be of good cheer, was a forced grin. His greenish eyes revealed no warmth, no inner life. His low voice, which he tried to mute even further (let us not forget that Bismarck, with whom he was claiming close resemblance, spoke very low) uttered nothing but predictable, colorless banalities, void of any real substance. Officials of the Third Reich were always required to have a witness at their side when they spoke to a foreign diplomat—for security reasons, no doubt (but was the concealed microphone not enough?). For that reason, the chief of protocol never ceased to be at my elbow. Neither he nor I got to hear anything very memorable. Ribbentrop confined himself to voicing his satisfaction at the good relations that reigned between our countries and his hope that, in these grave times, Romanians would rally around General Antonescu, in whom, in the aftermath of the previous month's upheavals, the German government had full confidence, valuing him both as a soldier and as a statesman. I asked in turn for Ribbentrop's cooperation during the performance of my difficult mission. I left the meeting chilled to the marrow, chilled to my very soul.

On the following day I was to meet the Führer and present to him the credentials from my monarch. A large car from the Reich's chancellery came to pick me up. I climbed into it along with the aide from the protocol office. Preceded and followed by other cars, we drove by the victory column, displaying its showy gild under a leaden sky. We glided down the Charlottenburgerallee, which bisected the Tiergarten and was not without a certain grandeur. We passed through the historic Brandenburg Gate and motored along Unter den Linden up to the Adlon—which, in those war years, enjoyed a monopoly in distinguished foreigners. Then we took a sharp right onto Wilhelmstrasse and—after driving by the British embassy, grave and menacing behind its closed shutters—we reached the new *Reichskanzlei,* whose architectural style (*Führerstil!*) clashed so unpleasantly with a square that, thanks to the palace built by Schinckel, retained an air of the past.

As if activated by automatic switches, huge gates swung open—first wooden ones, then others cast in iron—to let in our motorcade. Huge gates better befitting a fortress or a prison. One couldn't help recalling Dante's line: "*Lasciate ogni speranza, voi ch'entrate.*"[1] In this court akin to an ancient Egyptian burial chamber, an honor guard responded to a rasping command and presented arms to the king of Romania's represen-

[1]Abandon all hope, ye who enter here.

tative. Then at the top of the stairs were aligned this new court's dignitaries, headed by Meissner, the Reich's chancellery's everlasting minister, who had served under three heads of state since the fall of the kaiser.

With slow and very small steps, as if we were following a religious procession, we filed through an immense hall paved in marble. It took a long time and was probably intended to imbue the visitor with a requisite feeling of reverence. After a few moments of waiting in a side-parlor, I was brought into the regime's "holy of holies." Once again the chamber was large, far too large. These new dictators loved vast spaces: they worried neither about getting lost nor about looking puny in such expanses. On the wall, a monumental full-length portrait of Bismarck must have felt quite astonished to be in such company. At the other end of the room, almost too far to see, was located the Master's desk. He got up and, followed by Ribbentrop, who looked more like a little boy in his august presence, began to walk. . . . Making our way from opposite ends of this amazing personal office, our hikes eventually ended and we met in the middle. Long handshake. The royal letter that I brought passed from my hands into those of my fearsome interlocutor. In keeping with the centuries-old ritual, I conveyed to him my monarch's greetings and I was charged with conveying a similar message back to King Michael. Then I was motioned toward a sofa, a huge sofa—everything was huge here—in which I became ensconced or, rather, swallowed up. Next to it, Hitler was seated in a deep and wide armchair. Around us, on other sofas, seats, and armchairs were Ribbentrop, Meissner, Dörnberg, and a background assortment of reporters and photographers (every meeting with the Führer needed to be immortalized in this manner).

It was no longer a personal audience, it was the Areopagus in session. The monarchs who receive the credentials of foreign envoys grant them the honor of a private conversation, but Hitler received you surrounded by his entire general staff. Did he do that out of caution? Or out of a desire to let all his close followers partake of the manna that was to issue from his lips?

As soon as he was seated, the Führer held forth. It was a soliloquy, for there was no way I could get a word in edgewise. No, it was an oration, a *lengthy* oration. I took this opportunity to scrutinize the man who was declaiming it, the man of the day. What first struck me was that he looked like anybody else! This was a face I had seen thousands of times, not only in the portraits that Dr. Goebbels had been strewing about the world for years, but everywhere in Austria, on village roads, in the streets of Vienna, in each coffeehouse you walked into, in any train station. Unlike his Italian colleague's mask, Hitler's face lacked characteristic features and was even almost void of expression. He did not appear disagreeable, he looked ordinary—not stiff and starchy, as in his photographs. His manners were simple and affable, and every now and then one glimpsed an Austrian smile, hovering quickly around his blue eyes rather than on his lips.

A nagging question arose in my mind and took hold of me: was this truly Hitler? Like everyone else, I had heard rumors of doubles who, at certain times, stood in for the Führer. But no, I was not hallucinating. It really was he. In spite of the conversational setting of our exchange, a metallic resonance could be caught at times in his voice that was akin to the booming outbursts of his public speeches.

What was he saying to me? That General Antonescu had greatly impressed him and that he considered him the best-qualified person to take charge of Romania's destiny in present circumstances. He regretted that the Iron Guard movement was causing Antonescu such difficulties and hoped that all those young men would rally around the general and that all Romanians would help him in his arduous tasks.

Hitler then reviewed the overall picture of German policy in Southeastern Europe. The relations that the Reich sought to develop with the states located in that area were of a purely economic nature. Germany, as a primarily industrial country, needed to supplement its economic system by drawing on raw materials that regions of Southeastern Europe possessed and, moreover, could only sell to Germany, since Britain and France were amply furnished in this regard by their overseas colonies. The Führer's face glowed and he raised his voice a bit: "To say that we want to subjugate you economically would be as absurd as saying that you want to dominate us economically. To tell the truth, we Germans are more dependent on you than you are on us, for one can live without machines, if need be, but one cannot live without bread. To be sure, we have troops in your country. Yet our fondest wish is to withdraw them, both from Romania and from Bulgaria, and to replace them with a military commission—and even that for only a little while, believe me. Germany has no interest in spending great sums to keep troops in Southeastern Europe. Moreover, it needs all its servicemen in order to colonize the Polish territories that it has annexed and also certain zones in the West. This colonizing work will take a half-century, which means that Germany can afford no other preoccupations until then. For while a country can be conquered in a few months, you need decades to assimilate it and organize it. It would be utterly ridiculous to believe rumors that allege that I intend to take over the Balkans. My only wish is to have peace and quiet over there, so as to permit an acceleration of production."

His final sentence was: "I still believe that everything will be wrapped up within the year, for we are on the eve of major historical events." These words, intended to impress the Romanian government, marked the end of the audience.

On the way home, I could not help wondering: When a man like Hitler has attained his country's pinnacle of power and, for a while at least, has almost become the absolute master of continental Europe thanks to his military victories, what prompts him to think that it is necessary or useful to make highfalutin declarations that so flagrantly contradict real facts? In the cases of Austria, Czechoslovakia, and Poland, he had made solemn pledges that he subsequently broke. Yet at the time when he was making these promises, Austrians, Czechs, and Poles could delude themselves into believing that he would keep them. That was no longer possible in Romania's case. At the time when he was assuring it that he did not intend to "subjugate it economically" he had already enslaved it. Did he think that Romanian public opinion was unaware of the commercial treaty that, on March 23, 1939, he had imposed on us through the agency of his emissary, Wohltat, a treaty that seized all the economic potential of the country for the benefit of Germany? And that had been followed by negotiations carried out for him in a threatening tone by his economic agents, men like Neubacher and Clodius. (The latter, incidentally, wore a smiling good-natured demeanor that seemingly mitigated the exorbitant nature of his demands.) Did Hitler really imagine that these intimidations were not known by everyone in the streets of Bucharest? No, it is unlikely that he did. However, he had long been accustomed to asserting blatant untruths, without hesitation, just because they looked good in the picture, and he knew that no one would dare to contradict him now that he was the world's most powerful lord. Similarly, no one stood up to refute Nero when he proclaimed himself the greatest poet and artist of his day.

Several days later, on March 20, I drove to Wilhelmstrasse for the ritual round of official calls. I started with the secretary of state, Baron von Weizsäcker, a Swabian from Würtemberg and the son of a former premier in that little kingdom. A former navy officer, he had joined the German foreign service after World War I. His rather unctuous courtesy had gained him the sympathies of several members of the diplomatic corps, including Sir Nevile Henderson. People pitied him and especially his charming wife for their grief: they had lost a son on the Polish front in the early days of the war. Given his upbringing, this man probably did not approve of what was going on around him, but he had become part of the system and wanted to howl with the rest of the pack.

In his memoirs, Ulrich von Hassell accuses Weizsäcker of having broken off his friendship with former colleagues as soon as he sensed that they, headed by Hassell, wanted to counter the policies of Hitler and Ribbentrop in order to preserve peace and safeguard Germany's existence. Terms such as "cowardly" and "loutish character" often flow from Hassell's pen when he reports the attitude of "Ribbentrop's right hand" toward co-workers who were more independent or braver than he. But all that was a German concern, not a Romanian one.

During our first meeting Weizsäcker gushed with friendly remarks and wishes of well-being for my country. I replied that such a well-being rested on the country's inner peace, which depended of course on our own wisdom but also on securing calm at our borders. Weizsäcker commented that the only danger that might threaten Romania would be from the east, and that we were shielded in that respect by Germany's pledge. I responded by sharpening the focus of my remarks: to ensure that our borders remained calm, we needed not only military security but also peace in our hearts, a peace that my countrymen could not experience while four million of their kin groaned under foreign rule. This allusion to the loss of northern Transylvania—through the *Diktat* handed down on August 30, 1939, in Belvedere Palace—was so clear that my very cautious interlocutor embarked on a diversionary tactic. He assured me that German diplomatic efforts would strive to harmonize differences and coordinate interests in Southeastern Europe.

I called on Political Affairs Director Woermann, a timorous official who always left a door ajar at the back of his office when he conferred with me—doubtless in order to ensure that our conversations were witnessed and recorded by a concealed stenographer. He announced to me Yugoslavia's decision to join the Tripartite Pact between Germany, Italy, and Japan. He also informed me of an upcoming visit to Berlin by Bárdossy, the Hungarian foreign minister, who once had been Hungarian envoy in Bucharest. We spoke about Turkey, and he asserted that Ismet Inönü had sent Hitler a letter pledging that so long as he was not attacked he would not take action—yet he will not be attacked even if Germany launches an attack against Greece. Yugoslavia's participation in the pact will encourage Turkey to maintain its neutrality. Given its alliance with Britain, one could not ask for more.

German officialdom devoted several ensuing days to greeting Hungary's new foreign minister, and everyone traveled to Munich to celebrate the traditional friendship and alliance binding Berlin and Budapest together. In the toast he offered on March 21, Ribbentrop recalled that "the Führer is the statesman who, once Germany had risen again, smashed the chains of the Trianon Treaty in order to provide the Hungarian people with the *Lebensraum* to which they are naturally entitled." He underscored that "the Hungarian nation under the leadership of His Most Serene Highness Regent Horthy is ever more intimately joined to the Axis and was the first other country to join the Tripartite Pact between Germany, Italy, and Japan." Then he expressed his great satisfaction that "Germany and Italy have been able to mend the grave territorial injuries inflicted on Hungary by the Trianon Treaty." For his part, Bárdossy assured Hitler that "in line with the work of the late Count Csáky, my first duty, as I see it, will be to lead Hungarian foreign policy in the spirit of the Tripartite Pact."

The press echoed those sentiments. The *Völkischer Beobachter* observed that Magyar aspirations, potentially costly to her three neighbors, depended on Germany's power for their fulfillment, and the *Berliner Börsen-Zeitung* insisted that the common destiny of these two nations, their *Schiksalsgemeinschaft,* had always been grounded in deep historical and emotional bonds. All this put greater pressure on Romania and Yugoslavia, and forced them to become more dependent on the Axis.

I went to Wilhelmstrasse and expressed to Political Director Woermann, who seemed to be the only one not in Munich, the profound bitterness felt in my country in realizing that Romania had joined the Tripartite Pact only to be then told in official speeches by the Reich's leaders that the loss of northern Transylvania constituted "a redress of past wrongs." My interlocutor seemed caught off balance. Probably in order to comfort me, he began to criticize the stance taken by Bárdossy in refusing to reopen direct discussions with the Romanian government so as to review the chief points of friction between the two countries. The Hungarian foreign minister had also asked that the joint German-Italian commission on Transylvania be disbanded, and Woermann acknowledged that this request offered "eloquent proof that this commission is having to examine incidents mostly provoked by the Magyar side." I let him know that, even though this control agency had so far proved quite ineffectual, its abolition would produce catastrophic alarm both in Bucharest and among the million and a half Romanians who had been transferred to Hungarian rule.

As Romanian envoy, I had no call to stick my nose in all these love effusions between Germans and Magyars. I used the opportunity to perform my round of courtesy calls on other foreign envoys, my new colleagues. On March 24, following a heavy bombing attack (the first I had experienced in Berlin), I called on Monsignor Orsenigo, doyen of the diplomatic corps and my neighbor on Rauchstrasse. A bright, refined Italian, formerly nuncio in Budapest, he struck me as being perfectly conversant with Central European politics but equally determined to remain in the wings of the diplomatic scene in Berlin, since he probably feared that by stepping too far forward he might bring harm to German Catholics, already so oppressed by the Nazi regime.

Among other colleagues whom I got to know and with whom I had excellent relations during my Berlin assignment, I would cite first Frölicher, the Swiss envoy; Rickert, the Swedish envoy; Ciro de Freitas-Valle, the Brazilian ambassador and one-time envoy to Bucharest; Gerede, the Turkish ambassador; and Morrison, the U.S. chargé d'affaires. Greece was represented by Rizo-Rangabe, who had been in Berlin for many years and who was quite pessimistic about his country's near future. "Caught between the Italian army and the German army, which doubtless will soon attack us in spite of the declarations of love Hitler keeps sending us, Greece will succumb," he told me, "but it will fall with beauty!" My charming Yugoslav colleague Andrić, a poet and a man of wit, could not get over his country's decision to join the Tripartite Pact. We were both in the same fix, and we shared a long handshake. "I can no longer make heads or tails of the psychology of nations," he lamented. "The Greeks were supposed to be very cautious people, you Romanians were deemed a peaceful, easy-going race, and we Serbs were considered diehards through and through. What do we see now? The Greeks are turning into reckless heroes, you folks are bloodthirsty revolutionaries [an allusion to the Iron Guard uprising], and we Yugoslavs are a malleable nation that adapts to the German yoke. Wouldn't you say that the war has changed our national characters?" Italy was represented by the fashionable Dino Alfieri and Japan by Oshima, an inscrutable general.

My most interesting conversation was, naturally enough, with Dekanosov, the Soviet ambassador in Berlin. A European war, he told me, will inexorably spill over into the Balkans. Once that region is ablaze, the various countries within it will perforce have to take their stand. The ambassador concisely reviewed the situation in which each Balkan country found itself, and he said in conclusion that "Romania's position depends on its current interests, which are congruent with Yugoslavia's and diametrically opposed to Hungary's." When I reminded him of the sad fate to which were subjected the Romanians who had been severed from their fatherland, he wondered why the Axis powers could not compel the Budapest government to pursue a more humane policy vis-à-vis its Romanian ethnic minority. Dekanosov then spoke to me of my colleague and friend Gafencu, who was my counterpart in Moscow and whom he characterized as a "charmer." On parting, we promised to take up again this conversation, whose tenor and thrust I reported to Bucharest.

The meeting that gladdened me most—and also deeply moved me in the current circumstances—was the visit made to me, in greatest secrecy, by Fiša, who was counselor of the Czech legation in Budapest when I was there as Romanian envoy. I had been very fond of this likable colleague of my friend Kobr, and seeing him now in Berlin as a clandestine visitor, as a patriot hunted by the Gestapo, made a profound impression on me. In a few words, he whispered to me what life was like today in that splendid land, which not so long ago was the Republic of Czechoslovakia, my country's ally, now torn asunder and turned into a German "protectorate." Though the regime was less harsh than in Poland and famine had not yet broken out, methods of political annihilation were nevertheless broadly used against this nation, once proud of its independence and high standard of living. Native citizens were systematically removed from all key positions—whether in politics, administration, economics, or intellectual life—and those pilfered jobs were given to members of the occupying nation. What sustained the spirit of the heroic Czechs was their unimpaired faith in a future British victory: only that could save them from the sad fate of being forcibly Germanized within a few generations.

YUGOSLAVIA JOINS THE TRIPARTITE PACT

On March 25, in Vienna's graceful Belvedere Palace, where Hitler had succeeded in accomplishing all his sinister plans for Southeastern Europe, a new funeral rite took place. After the abolition of Czechoslovakia, after the enslavement of Romania, it was worn-down Yugoslavia's turn to submit to the German yoke. The beautiful eighteenth-century building designed by the great architect Fischer von Erlach, from whose windows you could see the wooded heights that rise above Vienna and the delightful terraced French gardens that Eugene of Savoy liked to stroll through, witnessed once again the heavy, crude silhouettes of the Nazi and Fascist leaders. Into the pearly gray atmosphere of the old imperial capital, suffused with grace, lightness, and balance, came strutting those morticians' uniforms, those gawky supposedly Roman salutes, those rasping, unpleasant voices—causing a strident contrast and tweaking nerves that were already on edge.

The opening assembly, presided over by Ribbentrop with Ciano on his right, was much like the unsealing of a last will and testament. On one side sat those who mourned in their hearts the passing away of old Europe, the survivors of the Little Entente: Romanians, Yugoslavs, and even Slovaks. On the other side fidgeted the impatient heirs who knew that the clauses of the will were all in their favor and who couldn't conceal their wicked glee: Nazis, Fascists, Hungarians, Bulgarians.

Draganov, the Bulgarian envoy—later destined to meet a tragic end at the hands of his countrymen—pointed his finger at Cvetković and Cinčar-Markovič, Yugoslavia's premier and foreign minister, both now in the hot seat, and whispered loudly and sarcastically: "Schauen Sie wie sie strahlend aussehen!"[2] The hapless representatives of Yugoslavia seemed shattered, in point of fact. They signed the piece of paper presented to them—it had already been presented to all governments of the Danube region—as if they were signing their own death warrants. It was their formal acceptance of the Tripartite Pact. However, there were two more protocols that had been concluded but were not read out. One was Germany's pledge to respect Yugoslav sovereignty and territorial integrity. (Italy had declined to sign this document, claiming that it had already given a partial pledge upon sealing the 1937 Italo-Yugoslav friendship pact.) The other protocol was Ribbentrop's formal promise, in the name of the German and Italian governments, not to transport troops through Yugoslav territory.

After the signing, Premier Cvetković rose to read a brief declaration in which he first affirmed that "Yugoslavia's chief goal—and, so to speak, her sole foreign policy goal—is to safeguard and reinforce peace on behalf of the Yugoslav people." Yugoslavia had therefore sought to normalize and improve its relations with her Italian, Hungarian, and Bulgarian neighbors. To this end "Yugoslavia associates itself to the Tripartite Pact; it does so to ensure a peaceful future . . . to attempt, above all, to prevent an expansion of the war." One could hardly have explained Yugoslavia's predicament more clearly: like Romania (its friend, neighbor, and ally), Yugoslavia saw itself compelled, under threat of war, to submit for the time being to the axiom that "might is right," while waiting for the day when might would realign itself with true right.

[2]"See how radiant they look!"

After that, we were obliged to listen to a long harangue by the Reich's foreign minister. It was a full-scale assault on Britain combined with hypocritical claims that everyone had ceased to believe long ago: "Germany solemnly declares that it pursues no territorial or political designs in the Balkans. Its present aim is merely to prevent a foreign power from seizing this space for purposes of prolonging the European war." On the way out, I walked near my Yugoslav colleague Andrić, my brother in misfortune, and I tried to raise his spirits: "You have still come out of this a little better than we did, whose territory they dismembered." Andrić replied, "Oh, you know, whether you twist or break your ankle, the result is the same." "Not really," I responded, "for a twisted ankle is easier to heal than an amputated foot."

Next came a gloomy luncheon in the exquisite setting of the Belvedere's circular Chinese room. It was presided over by the Führer, whose arrival was announced by three resounding knocks of a staff on the floor, as if he were a successor of the Austrian emperors, the masters of this place. The shades of Archduke Franz Ferdinand d'Este, last owner of the palace, and his ancestors must have shuddered then with indignation, and they must have done so again upon seeing Hitler, who never ate meat, attentively dice with his knife the vegetables served to him. Ciano and Mackensen felt obliged to select the same menu as their host, without however, wielding their knives. While we were being served wine, I saw the glass of the temporary master of this house get filled with a yellowish liquid. (Was it orangeade or syrup-flavored water?) The mood was lugubrious. The silence was oppressive, for Hitler was unable to communicate with those seated next to him, Oshima and Ciano: the three of them had not a single language in common. It truly was a funereal meal. The Yugoslavs made a pitiful sight. Did they already guess what would be in store for them when they returned home? They had managed to patch up their cabinet, almost overthrown by the crisis provoked by the prospect of the Tripartite Pact affiliation. Did they realize how fragile this patching up was?

We left the table. Cvetković and Cinčar-Markovič started to light their cigarettes, but an aide warned them that Hitler was allergic to cigarette smoke. I walked up to them. To them, as well, I said that their advantage over the Romanians was that they did not suffer cruel and unfair losses of territory as they were driven into subjugation. With a furrowed brow, the Yugoslav foreign minister replied, "I doubt that anyone in Belgrade will be grateful to us for that."

Portly Ciano pasted a falsely jovial look on his broad face and waddled in my direction. I stepped forward. He pulled me toward the recess of a window, relieved to find someone with whom he could talk among all these stiff-necked people who spoke nothing but German. He recalled the dinner I had hosted for him the preceding year in Rome, on the terrace of the Villa Ruspoli, residence of the Romanian legation. "Such a splendid view of the Eternal City from the heights of the Janiculum, the sweet-smelling spring evening, and your best Romanian caviar!" Not to mention the pretty women, who were a bit scarce at the Belvedere, now that the "dancing master" was Hitler instead of Eugene of Savoy. "Aren't you nostalgic for Italy? For my part, I begin to feel nostalgic as soon as I ride over the Brenner Pass. Why did you leave?" He added a few nasty remarks about my successor in Rome ("a revolutionary who refuses to learn diplomatic manners"), probably because he imagined this would please me.

I prosaically drew the conversation away from the pines of the Janiculum and the murmur of the Paola Fountain, to the harsh realities of the present hour. Ciano seemed discouraged. He believed that the war would continue for a very long time. In the meantime, one had to avoid anything that would bring about further complications, hence he would do all he could to make the Hungarians better disposed toward the Romanians in the part of Transylvania now occupied by them. I took the opportunity to remind him once again of the deep bitterness felt by all Romanians after the tragic amputation of their national territory in this same Belvedere. "Do not lose hope," he told me as he put his hand on my arm. "You know that Italy, too, had to relinquish Nice and Savoy, and that has not prevented it from becoming what it now is."

A few days later, on March 26, there was the official visit to Berlin of Matsuoka, the Japanese foreign minister. What had he come to tell his two Axis colleagues in Europe? Dekanosov, the Soviet ambassador, confided to me that Matsuoka had come "to put on the brakes, not to press on the gas pedal." On his journey home, he was to make a stop in Moscow, which Dekanosov viewed as a sign that relations between the USSR and the empire of the rising sun were improving. My Chinese colleague, on the other hand, was convinced that the head of the Japanese foreign service was promising to attack Singapore. It seemed likely that Matsuoka had come to check how the Axis was doing and to ascertain afterward, in Moscow, that Japan would not be attacked by Russia if Tokyo decided to launch a war against the United States. The fishing rights in Korea and the economic relations between Russia and Japan were only a pretext—a Japanese screen, as it were.

A great dinner took place that evening at the Esplanade Hotel. As it happened, I was seated close to Prince August Wilhelm of Prussia, first cousin of the Romanian queen mother. He told me how much he admired his aunt, Queen Marie of Romania—when he was three, he called her his "great flirtation." He also admired beautiful Queen Natalia of Serbia, Romanian by birth, whose picture could always be found on the desk of his grandfather, Wilhelm II—and that, he added, caused the empress to be jealous.

YUGOSLAV ABOUT-FACE; GERMANY ATTACKS YUGOSLAVIA AND GREECE

How soothing was this conversation, which took us miles away from the gloomy atmosphere that surrounded us. But now landed a bombshell—figuratively speaking, of course. Regent Paul of Yugoslavia has abdicated, Premier Cvetković and his foreign minister, Cinčar-Markovič, have been arrested for signing the Tripartite Pact. King Peter II has taken over the reins of power and has entrusted the government to General Simović, with Nincić as foreign minister. The Serbian military junta, which is blamed in Berlin for this "reversal of alliances," takes a pro-British stance, and anti-German demonstrations are swelling in Belgrade.

These events threw a pall over the warm meetings with Matsuoka. The Japanese foreign minister replied in very peaceful fashion to Ribbentrop's warlike speech. Both at this gala reception and at the next day's reception in the Japanese embassy, the head of Germany's foreign service disclosed his anger about the affront suffered by the Führer. He placed the blame more on the USSR than on Britain, a hypothesis seemingly confirmed in that the new Yugoslav cabinet included Gavrilović, recently Belgrade's envoy to Moscow. Every sentence uttered by Ribbentrop contained a threat against Yugoslavia. An attack against that country appeared imminent, and Sztojáy, Hungary's envoy, at once hastened back to Budapest. His Bulgarian colleague expected that the events that were unfolding would be very profitable to his country. Andrić had been urgently called home for consultations in Belgrade. During this commotion, Matsuoka's departure went unnoticed, as did most of his stay in Germany.

The contemplated attack against Yugoslavia had to be part of a bigger plan by the German general staff, for I learned that German troops had been reinforced along all sectors of the Russian border and that measures were being taken to evacuate German women and children from Polish districts close to the Soviet border. At the same time, it appeared that considerable numbers of ambulances and medical trains were being sent in the same direction. It goes without saying that I reported these facts to my government.

Hungary had decided to assist the German aggression against Yugoslavia with all its military means, in spite of the friendship pact that had just been sealed between Budapest and Belgrade, with its special nonaggression clause. But Paul Teleki, being the gentleman he was, was in despair and took his own life.

Since the plans provided for an attack on Yugoslavia by sending Hungarian forces through the Banat, part of which belongs to Romania, I received instructions from Bucharest to warn the German government that Romanian public opinion, already sickened by the loss of national territory to Hungary, would not accept this new injury and threat. If Hungarian troops were to enter Yugoslav Banat, Romania might be forced to intervene and drive them out. Ribbentrop replied to me, cautiously and reluctantly, that if an attack against Yugoslavia were ever to be contemplated (and all its details had already been mapped out!), the issue that I raised would pertain more to strategy than to foreign policy. He nevertheless took clear note of my statement.

I took this opportunity to lodge again a complaint about the treatment meted out by the Hungarian authorities on the Romanian population of northern Transylvania. The 130,000 Romanians driven out by these authorities were now refugees sheltering on Romanian territory and were being denied permission to return home. The land reforms enacted by the Romanian government after the last world war had been rescinded, and the peasants had been divested of their small landholdings in order to restore the vast feudal estates of Hungarian magnates. However, the Reich's impassive foreign minister led me to understand that he would not be able to concern himself with disagreements between Romanians and Hungarians until the Yugoslav problem had been settled. All the same, it appeared that my démarche had an effect, since the very next day Ambassador Ritter informed me, on behalf of his boss, that Hungarian troops would not be authorized to cross the border of the Yugoslav Banat.

During the night between April 5 and 6, without any declaration of war (of course!), German forces unleashed their offensive against Yugoslavia and Greece. In his general orders to the troops, Hitler enjoined them to use brutal force if necessary. Superfluous advice! Two hundred and fifty warplanes reduced Belgrade to ashes. Alfieri did not appear delighted. With a worried look, he told me his apprehensions. This German decision—taken unilaterally, he intimated—could entail heavy consequences for Italian troops in Albania, which will be caught in a crossfire and face serious risks, especially on account of the 200,000 British soldiers who had disembarked in Greece. I had the fairly distinct impression that Italy disapproved of this new military campaign, which it had wished to see delayed. I told Alfieri of my worry about what would ensue were the Hungarian troops to push up to the Romanian border in the Yugoslav Banat: tempers at home had already been chafed quite enough by oppressive measures against Romanians in northern Transylvania.

Yugoslavia had soon to capitulate, and the fate befalling that poor, heroic country seemed most tragic. Officials in Berlin did not conceal that the Kingdom of the Yugoslavs was doomed as a unitary state and would vanish. An independent Croatia was going to be established, but its fate would scarcely be more enviable and the Croats were going to be quite disappointed. Even though their country's crown was to be offered to the king of Italy or to princes of his family (the choice would actually fall on Duke Aimone of Spoleto, later duke of Aosta), they would find their territory radically trimmed on account of the Duce's inordinate ambitions: he was clamoring for the annexation of Slovenia, Dalmatia, and even, one way or another, Montenegro (there was talk of a restoration there of the Petrović-Niegoc dynasty, from which Queen Helena of Italy was descended). He wanted a territorial land bridge to Albania in order to become the unchallenged master of an Adriatic *mare nostro*.

Within the German government these immoderate demands produced astonishment and even indignation. The ethnic principle would be cynically and cruelly trampled, and—worst of all—this time it would take place to the detriment of pure-blooded Germans, such as the ones living in and around Laibach (Ljubljana), who would find themselves sharing the gloomy fate of their brethren in southern Tyrol. The Italian ambassador, however, bubbled with optimism about the future. All those sundry nations called into the paternal fold of Fascist protection had all been under Venetian rule at one or another moment of their history, had they not? Albania would expand in the direction of Macedonia and Epirus. The Bulgarians, for their part, demanded not only Greece's eastern Thrace but also Yugoslav Macedonia, up to the Albanian border and, northward, up to the Sar hills. The Hungarians, so well liked by the Germans, had their eyes on the Bačka region and the Yugoslav Banat. Finally, it seemed that Ribbentrop and Ciano would examine all these matters around April 20 in Vienna, where the Führer's headquarters were currently situated. It was the place where they habitually carved up their prey. Unfortunate Romania knew it all too well! King Boris and Horthy had already hurried to demand a share of the Yugoslav spoils on behalf of their respective country.

Given its current situation, Romania's government could of course not refuse to acknowledge an "independent" Croatia, but it was trying to delay as much as possible any official recognition or other sign of complicity. Bucharest was mindful of its old historical and dynastic ties to Yugoslavia, and also did not wish to provoke the USSR. I imparted that information to the political director, Woermann. I also asked him to see to it that captured Yugoslav servicemen of Romanian nationality did not fall into the hands of Hungarian or Bulgarian troops and, if possible, that they be allowed to return peacefully to their homes. I was notified a few days later that our requests would be taken into consideration, but I had no way of checking whether this promise was followed by actual deeds.

ON THE BRINK OF THE GERMAN-RUSSIAN WAR

German troops now occupied the island of Samothrace and this worried the Turkish government, for that island controls the entrance to the Dardanelles. Moreover, it was learned that German forces had been reinforced along Turkey's European border. Ambassador Gerede demanded an explanation from Wilhelmstrasse, but was told that none was required since the island of Samothrace belonged to Greece, not Turkey. Needless to say, this intimidation policy on the part of the German government caused tensions between these two old allies of World War I. Everyone was aware, in Berlin as well as Ankara, that the game would be closely played, for Turkey was the only country that still stood in the way of a German expansion into the Middle East.

Rumors of German troop movements on the Russian border continued to circulate. Curiously enough, the Italian ambassador, who after all should have been better informed than I about German intentions, asked me whether I did not have the feeling that the German government was planning an action against the USSR. Was Alfieri kept in the dark about Axis plans—as was Gafencu, my "opposite number" in Moscow—or was he trying to find out whether I had got wind of something? I replied that I was asking myself the same troubling question and had instructed my military attaché to make discreet inquiries around the German general staff; what he had obtained were categorical denials of the rumors afloat in Berlin's diplomatic quarters.

Here was a telling sign. In reply to my reports on that question, General Antonescu asked his secretary-general, Cretzianu, to send me and all other Romanian envoys abroad two instructions: desist from all further inquiries into Germany's eastern military plans, and send the foreign ministry no more reports or telegrams concerning German aggressive intentions against Russia.

Nonetheless, the breath of war against the Soviets was in the air and was the main topic of conversation among diplomats and foreign journalists; also by a strange coincidence, people spoke to me much more frequently than before about Bessarabia and northern Bukovina, the two Romanian territories annexed by the Soviet Union in June 1940. The speech Hitler was to deliver on May 4 at the Kroll opera house, where the National-Socialist pseudo-parliament had been meeting since the Reichstag was burned down, was feverishly awaited.

What did he declare in that speech? First he intoned his old refrain: the Reich had no political designs in Southeastern Europe, simply some economic interests. If he nevertheless decided to modify structurally the countries in that zone of the continent, it was not because he considered the old political configuration to be unfair. The proof of this was that Greece would emerge virtually intact from the conflict, and he had even been willing to respect Yugoslavia's territorial integrity, indeed awarding it the Salonika region. (What an interesting official declaration on the part of the Führer!) The reason for his decisions lay above all in the gratitude Germany owed Hungary and Bulgaria for their cooperation during World War I, and to Italy for its assistance in the current conflict. We thus learned for the first time, with some astonishment, that Hitler's political motivation was sentimental in nature. This revelation must have been startling to Austrians who still dared to think their own thoughts and recalled that their country had also been Germany's ally from 1914 to 1918.

There followed a warm aria about Hungary and an even more laudatory one about Bulgaria. Hitler patted himself on the back for achieving "the succesive revision of old treaties and unfair peace settlements" and for "righting past wrongs" on behalf of these two old and faithful allies, all of which had enabled Germany "to pay off an old historical debt of gratitude."

Croatia was barely mentioned at all, probably on account of the heavy sacrifices to which it would have to agree. Regarding Romania, he only praised the Conducător for his loyalty and for pursuing a "purely Romanian policy." The Serbs were given a really bad time. Fuming, Hitler blamed them for having allowed themselves to be led to disaster by "a gang of military conspirators." On the other hand, the artist he fancied himself to be waxed lyrical in speaking of "Hellas," his unrequited passion. He voiced several times his admiration for the heroic behavior of the Greek army—which he nevertheless did not hesitate to crush by means of numerical superiority. One got the impression that unfortunate Greece might perhaps escape the worst, thanks to the would-be Greek expert of Berchtesgaden. A few rhetorical flourishes were bestowed on Turkey, a former ally whom he invited, amiably if obliquely, to rejoin the German side.

In a passage of some significance Hitler spoke of improvements in weapons and equipment for German soldiers "this year and next." In other words, the war was no longer expected to end within the current year, as Hitler had consistently announced until now and as Ribbentrop had still recently predicted in his toast to Matsuoka.

But the most important point in the speech was probably the following sentence: "The German army will always decide where an attack has to be made and when it has to be launched." Hitler usually declared that the German army would go into action wherever British troops were to be found, but today he preferred not to specify the exact target of his future offensive operations. Could this mean that he had definitely decided to make war on Russia, and soon?

The German press had been instructed to publish lengthy commentaries on this speech. They underscored the passages concerning Hungary and Bulgaria, as if these two countries were to assume a pioneering role in the future expansion of German influence throughout the Danube Basin and the Balkans. The Hungarians had always played an important role in Germany and that was clear as soon as one arrived in that country. Its theaters, cinemas, and concert halls featured nothing but Magyar artists. Hungarian restaurants abounded everywhere. Newspapers kept praising the bravery and chivalrous attitudes of "our Hungarian brothers-at-arms" or of "the noble Magyar nation." That nation's recent territorial gains were all labeled "compensations for wrongs," even though German journalists, with their proverbial *Gründlichkeit,*[3] must have had a subtler understanding of the various ethnic problems at hand.

All this was due, first of all, to the fact that the Hungarians were purely Germanic in culture. A consequence of their many years under the Austrian monarchy was that, for any Magyar intellectual, German was his second mother tongue, if not perhaps his first. Whereas Romanians were imbued with French culture and thought as easily in French as in their own language, whereas for Bulgarians, Serbs, and so on, Russian was the language of the intellectual classes, Hungarians preferred to express themselves in German. It was the language used by families of

[3]Thoroughness.

the high society, including the Horthy family. A German who spoke with a Hungarian had the impression of talking with a countryman, so deep were the affinities of mind and culture between them. The military alliance between the two countries during the 1914 war was another factor; the generals of these two countries were in fact comrades-at-arms.

The Bulgarians also enjoyed feelings of solidarity with their old war partners, for they too, from 1914 to 1918, had shared the triumphs and then the setbacks of the German armies. More modest than the Hungarians, they did not hesitate to ascribe their recent political successes to Berlin's friendship, whereas the Hungarians invoked imaginary military victories. Bulgarophilia, rendered fashionable the preceding century by Gladstone, had turned into a German monopoly now that Ottoman persecutions had ceased and the "grand old man" had passed away. Thanks to King Boris's skill, the "Prussians of the Balkans" were coddled by the day's masters. The semi-official *Börsenzeitung* (in fact all German newspapers were semi-official), with Karl Megerle wielding his pen, lavished fulsome praise on "the greatest Balkan state of the future . . . , bordering henceforth not only the Black Sea but also the Aegean; from this new position, it is destined to play a major role, thanks to the political maturity of its people as well as Germany's friendship." That role consisted in becoming a Germanic bastion against a direct or indirect Anglo-Saxon penetration into the Balkans and in helping secure the lines of communication necessary for achieving the old "Berlin to Baghdad" dream of connecting the Reich to the Persian Gulf.

A certain sensation was caused in Berlin by Stalin's stepping into the role of Soviet premier. Wilhelmstrasse presented it as a sign of a rapprochement between Russia and Germany. A detail that seemed at first blush to confirm this interpretation was the authorization apparently granted by Moscow for Soviet volunteers to enroll in the Iraqi army during Iraq's uprising against British rule. When speaking to foreigners, German officials always had praise for the correct fashion in which Russians fulfilled their commitments to furnish raw materials to Germany. The Turkish side wondered whether the German government had not once again given the green light to Soviet ambitions in the direction of the Persian Gulf.

The greatest sensation those days was, however, Hess's flight to Britain (May 11). Several hypotheses were suggested: Hess fled because he thought that his life was in danger, owing to growing rivalry between the SS and SA, or perhaps he lost his wits because he realized that a German defeat was inevitable, etc. The most plausible explanation, however, which later events seemed to confirm, was that he was sent by Hitler in order to propose, one last time, a special, direct deal with Britain before unleashing his offensive against Russia. It is striking that no one accused Hess of being a traitor. The party line when his mission proved unsuccessful was to call him insane. Hence the following ditty that made the rounds:

Es geht ein Lied durchs ganze Land:
"Wir fahren gegen Engeland!"
Doch wer als erster dorthin fährt
Der wird gleich als verrückt erklärt![4]

Toward the end of May, it began to be rumored in diplomatic circles that, since the United States was likely to enter the war on the side of the Allies, the German government would try to clarify as soon as possible its relations with the Soviets. To that end, it envisioned asking Moscow for certain pledges that would ensure complete security for Germany on its eastern flank. This request would take the form of a veritable ultimatum, and the requested guarantees would be not only economic in nature but also military and territorial.

As a means of pressure, heavy reinforcements of German troops were massing along the Russian border and in Finland: that evidence could not be kept secret from travelers in trains and railway stations. The Wehrmacht was hiring interpreters left and right who knew Russian, Ukrainian, Latvian, or Estonian. Volunteers were recruited among Baltic refugees. I tried to confirm this rumor by consulting Woermann. He did not deny that military reinforcements were being sent eastward, but he assured me that they were merely a contingency plan for the Balkan campaign, to be ready for any surprise. As for the negotiations with Russia, he told me there neither were nor would be any. Regardless of what was being said, it did appear that German-Russian relations, one way or another, were approaching a decisive phase: either there would be a total mutual understanding, amounting to a takeover of the Soviet Union by Hitler, or there would be a war unleashed by the Führer for the same purpose.

To carry out the great events that he was plotting, Hitler needed to keep discontent at a minimum on his borders. It was a delicate moment for Germany, and France hoped to take advantage of it in order to obtain a reduction of the payments to the Reich that had been crushing it ever

---

[4]A song sweeps throughout the land:
"We're moving against England!"
Yet he who moves there double quick
Will soon pass for a lunatic.

since the armistice. Darlan came to Berchtesgaden on May 10, but it looked as if concessions would once again be forced on hapless France. Darlan had to turn over strategically valuable Syrian airports to the German armed forces in exchange for a vague promise of lowering the daily payments of 400 million francs that the French treasury had to pay for the costs of the German occupation troops.

Several less busy days gave me the opportunity of revisiting Prague, that jewel of medieval art and advanced center of Czech technology, now reduced in rank to "capital of the protectorate of Bohemia and Moravia." I paid a call on our legation there, also reduced in rank to consulate general, which was housed in one of the city's most beautiful baroque buildings, the Czernin-Morcsyn Palace. Those sunny June days, perfumed with springtime odors, made the fate of Prague and Czechoslovakia stand out in tragic contrast. The German masters were systematically seeking to destroy this admirable nation. The Czech language was methodically suppressed. Street signs placed the Czech names below their German equivalents. The penalty for a small student demonstration had been the execution of the nine student union presidents and closure of the university for three years. German tourist guidebooks proclaimed that Prague was a German city, even though scarcely 10 percent of its inhabitants were of Germanic stock, and contained insulting sentences such as this: "The Ständetheater, built by Count Nostitz, was degraded into a Czech theater from 1920 to 1939."

All key positions in the economic sphere were given to Germans. The directors of the largest Czech bank, *Zivnostenska Banka,* had been arrested under various pretexts and replaced by Germans. Statues of Czech patriots had been dismantled and replaced on their pedestals by likenesses of Germans or Austrians (such as Radetzky). German soldiers on leave and groups of schoolchildren descended like locusts and were placed in Czech villages in order to be fed, although they were forbidden to "fraternize" with the native population. Count Borek-Dohálsky, a dear friend and former colleague of mine in Vienna, who would die as a martyr in Dachau along with his brother the bishop, told me that, unless halted by an Anglo-American victory, the occupiers would pursue their assimilation policy with satanic zeal and in ten years' time there would no longer be a Czech nation. Yet, he added with glistening eyes, all Czechs were convinced that right and liberty would triumph over brutal force.

I returned to Berlin, where rumors of a German eastward offensive were growing. The Germans wanted to wrap up the discussions about Yugoslavia as quickly as possible before leaping into the great adventure.

Hungary, their future "associate" in the Danube Basin, had first to be assuaged, and Hitler called upon the Croats to relinquish the Bačka region to it. Hungary would also be given the Serbian Banat. Bulgaria would receive Macedonia, Eastern Thrace, and the islands of Samothrace and Thasos. The eastern half of the Balkan peninsula would become a German zone of influence (Romania, Serbia, Bulgaria, Hungary) and the western half an Italian zone (Croatia, Slovenia, Dalmatia, Montenegro, Albania).

After King Boris and Pavelić, General Antonescu had been summoned to Munich on June 11 and our foreign ministry's secretary-general telephoned me to request that I be there for his arrival. But I was not present at the actual discussions between the Conducător and the Führer. Ribbentrop and several generals were reportedly included in some of them. Our ministry's political director, Davidescu, told me he overheard Hitler exclaiming that there were only two men he could count on outside of Germany: Mussolini and Antonescu. The beaming faces of the officials indicated that they were looking forward to major events—if not with a light heart, then at least with complete optimism.

The Germans and the Turks signed a pact on June 18. Berlin considered that Ankara had now joined the "friends of the Axis" club. Turkish-British friendship continued, but it was mitigated by Ankara's pledge not to undertake any action that could be harmful to Germany. Were secret meetings being held? Rumor had it that there might be a border revision in Eastern Thrace to the detriment of Bulgaria.

From Moscow, Gafencu informed me that his wife and the spouses of all other members of his legation would return to Romania via Berlin, where they would arrive on June 21. My worst fears were thus confirmed. If with great urgency my friend Gafencu had decided to send to me all the ladies of his legation (and especially his own wife) in a special plane, the reason must be that his German colleague, Count von der Schulenburg, had forewarned him of an imminent German attack on Russia. Romanian forces would have to participate in such an attack, since the Russian invasion of Bessarabia and northern Bukovina the previous year obliged Romania to follow the course set by the Third Reich, if it wished to maintain a modicum of independence and escape Poland's tragic fate. Accompanied by my wife I went to Tempelhof airport to greet the wives of our colleagues in Moscow, who had arrived by the last available plane, as they told us. Our friend Edmée Gafencu was distressed by the great drama that, she knew, was about to unfold. She told me that her husband considered the Red

Army very powerful and did not rule out surprises. In any case, he feared that there would be famine and indescribable chaos, for it would take the Germans a long time to turn the Ukraine into an organized entity. Mrs. Gafencu stayed with us at the legation. We found lodgings for the other women in nearby hotels.

THE GERMAN-RUSSIAN WAR

On June 22, I was awakened at 3:45 A.M. by a telephone call from the *Auswärtiges Amt*[5] telling me that the foreign minister wished to see me in three-quarters of an hour. At half past four, on the dot, I walked into the Wilhelmstrasse offices, where I also found my Finnish and Hungarian colleagues. One after the other, we were taken into Ribbentrop's office. He was stiffer and more solemn than ever, and his features were drawn from lack of sleep. In a voice that nevertheless trembled slightly (or so it seemed to me), he informed me that an hour and a half earlier—that is, at 3:00 A.M.—he had handed a note to Dekanosov, the USSR ambassador, in which the German Reich declared itself in a state of war with the Soviet Union. Hostilities had begun at that very moment: on June 22, at 3:00 A.M. "The war will be no picnic," he added, "for Slavs make good soldiers. But your troops and ours will win!" Handshake. That was it.

I left, feeling deep turmoil. We were at war: a tremendous war this time, and I had just heard it confirmed—by the Reich's foreign minister, no less—that my country's troops were fighting alongside Germany's in order to retake that Bessarabia and northern Bukovina which a threatening ultimatum had torn away from us a year ago, almost to the day. I returned to the legation, where Edmée Gafencu and my wife were awaiting my return, suspecting what had occurred. The prospect of seeing our country able (God willing) to recover the cherished provinces that had been torn away from it did not dispel our fears and worries about the future. No one could believe, deep down, that Hitler would achieve a permanent victory. A religious service was held in the Romanian chapel to pray for divine blessing over our country and our armed forces at this grave time. We all attended—Mrs. Gafencu, my wife and I, and the members of our legation.

Mrs. Gafencu was understandably very worried about her husband in Moscow. The Bulgarian government, now overseeing our interests in the

[5] Foreign Office.

USSR, could not at first establish contact with our embassy in Moscow. It was finally decided that the exchange of diplomatic personnel would take place on the Turkish-Russian and Turkish-Bulgarian borders.

The Turko-German pact of June 18, 1941, was to assume the same role during the 1941 German-Russian war as had been played by the pact of August 23, 1939, between Berlin and Moscow during the war unleashed by Hitler on September 1, 1939, against France, Britain, and Poland. In the earlier case, the aim had been to neutralize Russia in order to avoid a war on two fronts. In the present case, the aim was to neutralize the last neighbor of the Soviet Union whose attitude could raise doubts.

But now Hitler was committing his big blunder, the fatal blunder that contained the seeds of the Reich's inescapable defeat: he was waging war on two fronts, the very thing that up to now he had always—and with good reason—sought to avoid. To shield himself from the tremendous risks he was taking, he attempted to turn his war into an anti-Communist crusade. The Anti-Comintern Pact, which had been shoved under the rug for close to two years, was brought back into force. In peremptory fashion, Italy, Finland, Hungary, and Romania were asked to sign along. Vichy France, Denmark, Slovakia, and Croatia had to sever relations with Moscow. Symbolic battalions from Spain, France, Denmark, Norway, and the Netherlands joined this Hitlerian crusade. Sweden also participated, in a sense, since it was forced to let German troops cross its territory from Norway into Finland. Even Portugal published anti-Soviet newspaper articles.

Unfortunate Romania also had to agree to heavy economic sacrifices. It had to send all its exports to Germany without being compensated either in German goods or in the hard currency that would enable it to buy goods elsewhere. This resulted in frozen credits in our favor amounting to 250 million Reichsmarks, a surplus that would rise to even more dizzying heights. When I discussed this with Clodius, the "maid of all works" for the wartime German economy, he told me that this credit was a splendid advantage for us, since after the final victory the Reichsmark would replace the U.S. dollar and possibly even the gold standard! After the victory! In the meantime, we had to pay for the German troops that were occupying the country (to that end our national bank had just been charged two billion lei), and we calmly had to watch our economic structure collapse. The Romanian state was even being asked to extend to the German army whatever sums it required in Romania, with no credit limit. This was an unprecedented demand, and I objected to it with all my might.

✧ ✧ ✧

At the end of August two full years had elapsed since the beginning of World War II, and there was no end in sight. The Germans had very great military victories on their scorecard but food restrictions were hitting them hard, and hitting equally all social classes in the Reich, it must be noted. The country's entire industrial production was being placed at the exclusive disposal of the war machine. Factories were now producing neither cars, nor radios, nor cameras, nor record players, nor leather goods, and almost no pharmaceuticals or tobacco. Smokers lined up for hours on end in front of tobacco shops. Failing means of transport prevented cities from being adequately provided with potatoes, fruit, and meat. For lack of personnel, tailor shops, dressmakers, and linen suppliers could no longer fill customers' orders. Only families with children were permitted to have servants. It was surprising to see how, without demur, the population accepted all these sacrifices imposed by the great warlord. There is no doubt about it: thanks to their innate discipline and passive compliance, the German people are the easiest in the world to rule.

On the international scene, German relations with Turkey seemed to be improving further. The Turkish foreign ministry's secretary-general, who had arrived to seal the recently agreed-to friendship pact between Berlin and Ankara, had just held negotiations that proved very fruitful, it was said. Conversely, Clodius was now in Ankara with numerous experts in order to sign a commercial treaty. Gerede, the Turkish ambassador, denied rumors that von Papen was pressuring his government to grant Axis warships (especially Italian) free passage through the Dardanelles under the cover of Bulgarian flags, and to allow German troops bound for Syria to transit through Turkey. Ribbentrop, it seemed, had reiterated to the Turks what he had said in his speech honoring Matsuoka: Germany's victory would be achieved before year-end. The Turks, however, were skeptical. Britain, in turn, would have liked to see them participating in *its* military actions.

The United States was clearly preparing to enter the war on Britain's side. The military draft law had been enacted. Germany's consulates were closed down and military bases were secured in Iceland. During the opening of a new wing of the Norwegian legation in Washington, Undersecretary of State Sumner Welles went so far as to state that "there will be no peace in Europe until the Hitler regime is completely and permanently destroyed in Germany." My American colleague did not hide from me that his days in the Reich's capital were numbered and that he and his co-workers were ready to leave "at a moment's notice."

The South American republics were following the same track. The government of La Paz had asked the German envoy, Wendler, to leave Bolivia within three days for having plotted against the security of that state in collusion with the revolutionary commander Belmonte. The Buenos Aires government had seized three rather suspicious diplomatic mailbags originating from the German legation in Peru and in transit through Argentina.

In China, the Axis powers recognized the puppet government in Nanking and severed relations with the one in Chungking. Consequently, the likable Chinese ambassador and all his personnel departed from Berlin, to the delight of the Japanese.

Meanwhile, military operations continued against the Soviet Union. Romanian troops retook Bessarabia and northern Bukovina. Romanian officers who were passing through Berlin told me that General Antonescu was outraged by the massacres of Bessarabian Jews committed by the Germans.

The prospect of an eastward territorial expansion was being dangled before General Antonescu as a way of enticing him to push beyond the Romanian people's legitimate and natural frontiers and to keep advancing farther in order to help the German offensive. The idea originated in Budapest, where it was hoped that Transylvania could be swapped for a so-called Transdniestria. The latter was an essentially Russian province, which was supposed to make up to the Romanians for the loss of Transylvania and to give them a place in which to relocate three million Romanians uprooted from Transylvania. I pointed out that maneuver to Bucharest: "Is Romania an oriental state [I wrote on August 5], when the Romanian people are western in origin and moral outlook, when the birthplace of their race lies at the foot of the Transylvanian Alps, when all their outlooks and inclinations lean toward the west? The extravagant hypothesis of a forced and massive migration of millions of Romanians from the Carpathians to the Russian steppes is a way of condemning Romania in advance. . . . Yet the *Rumänien-Oststaat* formula is considered by several high officials of the Auswärtiges Amt to offer a possible and rather tempting solution to the centuries-old conflict between Romanians and Hungarians. . . . If Romania's center of gravity were to shift eastward it would perhaps also be a way of getting Romanians to accept the idea that, in exchange for compensations in the east, Transylvania and the Banat will be turned into an autonomous state governed by the Germanic section of its population. . . . This explains why we are constantly being pushed eastward, while our rights in the west and our aspirations there are ignored. All this can only arouse apprehension in our hearts. Since this question is being discussed within the foreign ministry and is being repeated by all organs of the (controlled) press in this country, I believe that we have the right—and we must use it—to declare firmly and openly that we will not renounce our historical place and role, such as they have been assigned to us by history and our geographical position."

✧ ✧ ✧

The continuing war held certain surprises for Hitler: increased resistance on the part of the Russian forces, Anglo-Russian penetration into Iran, a meeting between Churchill and Roosevelt on board the USS *Potomac*, followed by the eight-point declaration of the Atlantic Charter. General discouragement settled over Berlin. People no longer deluded themselves as to how long the war would last, even if they still trusted the outcome. Mussolini was urgently summoned to the Führer's headquarters in the first days of September, for the two dictators had to consult each other on what course to set. They announced that they intended to destroy bolshevism and that they would not intervene in Turkey, unless that country embraced the Allies or gave in to their pressures, which did not appear likely. Gerede in Berlin and von Papen in Ankara both seemed convinced that Turkey was unswervingly committed to repelling any foreign interference with armed force.

Germany wished to acquire air and sea bases in North Africa so as to organize from there a naval confrontation with Britain. But for that to work out it would have been necessary to reach an official peace with the Vichy government. That, in turn, would only have been feasible if the idea of taking away part of France's metropolitan territory had been abandoned. Hitler, however, coveted Alsace and Lorraine. The Duce, too, in spite of his crony's suggestions, persisted with his territorial demands over Nice, Corsica, and Savoy.

A few days later it was Horthy's turn to come to Germany. He arrived at Hitler's headquarters with his premier, Bárdossy, and the Hungarian chief of staff, General Szombathaly. The Hungarians were rescinding the Romanian agrarian reforms that had enabled Romanian and Hungarian peasants to own the small plots they tilled; they massed troops on the Romanian border, and my colleague in Budapest could not obtain an appointment to see the head of government. Horthy was said to be asking for the restoration of St. Stephen's kingdom or, at least, the return of the Serbian Banat, as an inducement toward intensified war efforts.

I talked about all this with the Italian ambassador, but his official optimism did not abet an exchange of ideas. The good Alfieri believed that "the war against Russia will be concluded by next spring" and would be followed by "a clarification of the Middle Eastern situation" plus an "invasion of Britain." Since he viewed life through rose-tinted lenses, he added that "it is not beyond the realm of possibility that all these operations will be achieved in 1942." I looked him straight in the eyes and asked, "*E tutto questo nel 1942?*"[6] A bit nonplussed, he hesitated, then weakly reiterated, "*Si, tutto questo nel 1942.*" He conceded, though, that if it proved otherwise, social unrest might break out almost anywhere among fatigued, disappointed peoples—in Serbia, Hungary, France. He also said he was aware of certain discontents in Romania, which clustered around the person of Maniu. I told him that these dissatisfactions would keep increasing if there was no redress to the injustices caused by the Belvedere *Diktat* on northern Transylvania.

This fact was confirmed to me by Archduchess Ileana, who spent a few days with us after returning from Bucharest. The Germans, she told me, were strongly disliked, and no one saw the point of continuing to wage war on the Russians now that Bessarabia and northern Bukovina had been recovered.

But the Transylvanian question was still what caused the most resentment. Under the pressure of public opinion, the government in Bucharest instructed me and my colleague in Rome to present a diplomatic note listing all the Hungarian authorities' grievous violations of the pledges they had made in Vienna. Their systematic persecution of the Romanian ethnic majority in the annexed province, their expelling of the Romanian intellectual elite, their rescinding of the agrarian reform, their further invalidation of voluntary land sales by Hungarians to Romanians—all those flagrant violations of the declaration of August 30, 1940, constituted a repudiation of that declaration on the part of the government in Budapest, and we took formal note of this. Weizsäcker, to whom I handed this diplomatic note, did not want to acknowledge in any way that their cherished *Diktat* had become null and void, and he alleged that he could not make out what I was saying. I replied that it was declared null and void by Hungary and not by Romania—even though we would have been justified to do so—for never before in history, except after a war

[6]And all that in 1942?

fought and lost, had a territory been taken away from the state to which the majority of its population ethnically belonged and given to a country whose nationals there were a minority.

The secretary of state for foreign affairs got hot under the collar. He told me that what went on in our hearts did not come under his purview. All that he requested was that neither Romanians nor Hungarians bring up with him the Vienna arbitration if their purpose was to undermine this instrument that mediated between the interests of the two nations. Did we, in the midst of a world war, want to start a private Romanian-Magyar war? I ought to be aware, chided Weizsäcker, that Germany's fondest wish was to find a formula for Transylvania that would equally content Bucharest and Budapest; however, in spite of all the efforts being made by Ribbentrop, Woermann, and himself, such a formula had not yet been found.

Yet Romania knew how to moderate its aspirations and even how to make sacrifices for the sake of maintaining harmony in Southeastern Europe. Thus, even though at the start of Germany's attack against Yugoslavia, General Antonescu had been invited to occupy militarily the area of the Banat awarded to Yugoslavia in 1919—and such an occupation might have secured him rights over the region—he had categorically refused to invade the territory of a state allied to Romania for the past twenty years.

Any offer of new territory—especially the offer of letting Romanians themselves select their eastern boundaries—was merely intended to compensate them for eventually losing all of Transylvania. In a conversation on October 9, I made it clear to Luther, foreign undersecretary, that Romanians would never accept losing Transylvania, whatever the price of that despicable barter. Never would we consent to uproot Transylvania's Romanians and relocate them beyond the Dniester. My point of view did not surprise Luther, who acknowledged that it was shared by all my countrymen. "In fact," he told me, "the Führer, wishing to demonstrate his feelings for Romania, invited General Antonescu himself to draw on the map what should be Romania's eastern border, pushing them as far to the east as he would judge appropriate. To Hitler's great surprise, the Romanian conducaˇtor merely asked for the old 1939 border, around Bessarabia and northern Bukovina—a very modest request!"

Rosenberg, who already envisioned Russia carved up into separate pieces, also spoke to me, on October 11, of the "vast expanses" that Romania could permanently acquire on its eastern flank, if it so wished. I replied to him, as I did to all those who sounded me along those lines, that "our eyes are only drawn in the direction of the territories where our ethnic brothers have fallen under foreign domination."

When northern Bukovina had been retaken and Romanian refugees were returning home there, the Nazi authorities tried to intersperse them with ethnic Germans who supposedly came from that region. I objected with all my might to the arrival of this potential fifth column, at a time when some officials desired to uproot the Romanian natives of northern Transylvania and relocate them on the Russian steppes. I encouraged my government to take a clear official stance on this issue, in order to put an end to the feverish fantasies that were sprouting within certain minds in Berlin and Budapest. Meanwhile, those generous Nazis were turning down the requests of General Jienescu, our air force undersecretary, who was asking them for planes to replace those that the German general staff had asked us to sacrifice.

✧ ✧ ✧

The good Alfieri continued to float in a cloud of complete and unaccountable optimism for the Axis. One could see that the dream of an easy armed stroll through Russia had been dispelled, yet on October 13 he was still telling me that the Soviet army would be beaten, though not destroyed, by wintertime. Moscow and Leningrad would fall soon, but the Caucasus would only be reached in the spring; after that would come simultaneous attacks against the Suez Canal and Gibraltar, as well as "a veritable submarine offensive that could seal Britain's defeat in 1942 and, of course, topple Churchill from power in London." Himmler, he added, was apparently convinced that he could quell any movement in Germany or in the occupied countries that might weaken the interior front. Draganov, the Bulgarian envoy, was more realistic; he foresaw unceasing resistance by the Soviets with Anglo-American help, the landing of American forces in Dakar, and serious conflicts between Italians and Slavs in the Balkans.

DANISH INTERLUDE

From October 15 to November 1, my wife and I spent a delectable, restful fortnight in Denmark, where I had also just been accredited as envoy. After the horror of Berlin and wartime Germany, this smiling oasis revived our spirits. We visited Sjaeland, and especially Köge and Roskilde—Denmark's royal abbey—before reaching charming Copenhagen. I had a meeting with Scavenius, the Danish doyen of all ministers of foreign affairs, since he already held his office during World War I. I had met him in the days of the League of Nations. An intelligent man and a liberal, he was said to be a friend of Germany—but of the old Germany, not that of the Nazis. In a splendid ancient coach and with very ancien régime court etiquette, I was led into Kristianborg Palace to present my credentials to King Christian X. He was very tall (six foot four), most distinguished, and wore across his chest a sash of the Order of Carol I. After the customary exchange of courtesies, the monarch complained about the German occupation of his country in flagrant violation of the nonaggression pact sealed on April 9, 1940. After six hours of armed struggle an agreement had been reached to determine the terms of occupation. "Whenever they fail to respect them," the king told me, "I am here, I protest, I remind them of their pledges." I expressed my admiration for his dignified attitude and his prestige, thanks to which one noticed in his capital "not so much the occupation forces as the presence of the king." "That is why," said he, "I do not leave Copenhagen for a single day. I need not tell you how impatiently I await the day when those people will pack up and leave."

I reminded my royal interlocutor of his triumphal journey to Paris in spring 1914, on the eve of the war. I was then a young student, and I saw him passing along the avenue du Bois next to Poincaré. "How long ago that all seems!" Very graciously, Queen Alexandrina deigned to receive my wife and me. We had, alas, to leave this enchanting country, since my thankless tasks in Berlin did not allow me to prolong this soothing respite.

BACK IN BERLIN

Back in Berlin, I was visited by Brandsch, leader of Transylvania's Saxons, who told me how he had refused to go along with Count Bethlen's attempts, under instructions from Count Welczek (the German envoy in Budapest and future ambassador in Paris), to seal a Magyar-Saxon pact against the Romanian regime in Transylvania.

Grim Hungarian oppression continued in the northern part of Transylvania. Abusive campaigns against the Eastern Orthodox Christians (that is to say, the Romanians), arrests, confiscations of property: they tried every trick in the book in their attempt to uproot the Romanians of Transylvania and relocate them beyond the Dniester—that bizarre and crazy idea with which Budapest's rulers were obsessed.

A Romanian economic commission arrived in Berlin at the beginning of November. Its leader, Minister of Economic Affairs Marinescu, explained to me our situation: we were the coerced creditors of the Germans to the tune of 300 million Reichsmarks. Nevertheless, they refused to furnish us the tractors and weapons that we needed, and moreover they demanded that we supply them with our entire production of cereals and petroleum, on credit naturally.

Diplomatic quarters and the foreign press were zestfully commenting upon two truly stupefying lectures. The first was a talk given by Frank, governor general of Poland and president of the German Legal Academy. He sought to prove that Poland was a German land not only by right of conquest but also historically and culturally. According to him, Poland's territory would have been originally Germanic, and to bolster this strange theory he spoke of Germanic swords discovered in Poland during recent excavations. He also unearthed a Germanic root in the name of every Polish scientist. This sickening contempt for historical truth would have caused laughter had it not been followed by the gruesome statement, "There will never again exist a Polish state." Did Frank remember his deplorable prophecy when he mounted the scaffold?

The other lecture—identical in outlook, actually—was given by Seyss-Inquart, the Reich's commissioner for Holland. The Netherlands, he alleged, were an integral part of Germany and "there will never again be an independent Dutch state." One wonders what the point was to all that bluster, when the chances of a total German victory must have looked quite problematic to people like Frank and Seyss-Inquart, who were privy to the secrets of the devil, rather than of the gods.

MIHAI ANTONESCU'S VISIT TO BERLIN

On November 25 the Romanian deputy prime minister, Mihai A. ("Ică") Antonescu, arrived in Berlin to sign the renewal of the Anti-Comintern Pact along with the representatives of other Axis-dominated powers. I met him for the first time face to face. He made a mediocre impression and, in Oriental fashion, he had brought too many gifts for his hosts, even though when he had sounded me out about this, I had said he should not do so. Nevertheless, here were caviar tins, pralines from Capşa, rugs, and icons (mostly Russian, by the way). Mihai Antonescu seemed lacking in experience and full of rather naïve optimism. His first meeting was with Ribbentrop, who affected an air of "British aloofness," but whose palpable lack of social ease betrayed his humble origins and inferiority complex. The "von" he had arbitrarily tacked in front of his name had apparently not brought along the refinement and style needed to act as the Metternich of what he envisioned to be a new Congress of Vienna, or to rise as the Congress of Berlin's Bismarck, which he conceitedly fancied himself to be.

Ciano, the first Axis partner, had become fat and bloated, and showed none of his usual exuberance. His retinue, on the other hand, exhibited a joyousness quite out of keeping with Italy's current situation. Hungary was represented by Bárdossy, pale and thin as a knife blade, Spain by Serrano Suñer, Slovakia by Tuka, who had a bishop's face and looked old and worn down by his nine years of imprisonment under the Czechoslovak regime. Popov was the classic Bulgarian, even though he was of Romanian origin (he spoke flawless Romanian), a bit unpolished but a realist. He had studied in Bucharest and later returned there as Bulgarian envoy. Larković, Croatia's foreign minister, was only thirty-two years old. Witting represented Finland, whose foreign minister he was. I had had excellent relations with this frank and direct man during my years as an envoy in Helsingfors. He was accompanied by the likable Raphael Hakkarainen, forever chief of protocol. We had a long talk together. Witting was no happier than I to find himself in such company. He said he was willing to join in a war against the Bolsheviks but was deeply distressed that this might have to entail a state of war with the Anglo-Americans. Scavenius, Denmark's foreign minister, was refined and distinguished, and did not hide from me that he shared the feelings of his Finnish colleague.

Mihai Antonescu had a meeting with Hitler. He thanked the Führer for help given to Romania so as to enable it to recover the territories lost after the Russian ultimatum of 1940. He asked for continued assistance in order that the country may be rebuilt, and to this end he asked him to support our country's fight against inflation and to curb Hungarian acts of aggression. Hitler replied with assurances of friendship toward Romania and its current leader, Field Marshal Ion Antonescu. Out of loyalty for the field marshal, he had broken off all ties with the Iron Guard, whose present leader was of lesser caliber than his predecessor, Codreanu. Sima had declined to come to Berlin—it was a telling sign. For Hitler, there was only one man who counted in Romania: Ion Antonescu. On the issue of economic relations, he had to insist on the need to increase Romanian cereal exports to Germany, for he had to take care of other countries, such as Finland. He also asked for additional efforts in the oil fields, efforts stretching over no more than two years, for Britain would certainly be toppled by then. As for German troops in Romania, which were the principal cause of inflation, they would be withdrawn in stages. Regarding Hungary, he had had to grant it advantages to the detriment of Romania, in order to maintain peace in that sector of Europe. But he had once warned a Hungarian: "Do not always speak to me of Hungary's thousand-year history; otherwise, I in turn will begin to talk of Germany's thousand-year history, and then you will be incorporated into the Reich!" "Those are people," he added, "who insist fanatically on rights that probably do not belong to them." He also alluded to territories that would eventually be granted in the east to compensate our country for its loss of Transylvania. He also stated for the first time the view that the presence of people belonging to one's race in another region did not provide sufficient grounds for annexing that region.

On November 28, our king and his mother arrived in Berlin and had a luncheon with the Führer, but I was not present at their discussions.

AMERICA IS SWEPT INTO THE WAR

December 7. Japan attacked today the Philippine Islands and Hawaii. The European War now becomes a World War.

December 12. America has gone to war. The "satellite" countries are forced, under compelling threat, to consider themselves at war with the United States. Pressures were brought to bear on Turkey in order to convince it to cross the Rubicon. It was invited to annex a swath of Syria extending from Aleppo all the way to the Mosul region, and it was promised the autonomy of all Muslims in the Caucasus. The Spaniards were lured with talk of operations in Gibraltar and Morocco. Göring had a meeting with Pétain in order to mollify him and obtain his active cooperation. But the talks were inconclusive, since he offered concessions neither on the issue of Paris nor on the question of the return of war prisoners. Ribbentrop and Ciano went to Budapest—and only to Budapest—to confer with Horthy and his cabinet.

The German government was informed, toward the end of January 1942, that during Eden's recent visit to Moscow the Soviets had apparently made the following demands: reinstatement of their 1941 borders and the right to station garrisons in Bulgaria, over which Russia would henceforth enjoy a "right of protectorate." The latter demand (already presented to Hitler by Molotov during his visit to Berlin), would have logically entailed a right of access through the Dobrudja. In addition to ancient wishes expressed in Berlin, Stalin also demanded the departure of the Bulgarian royal family, the establishment of a republic in Sofia, the right to oversee the Dardanelles straits, and a zone in Iran. He appeared, this time around, to have conceded the possibility of creating a new independent Poland, but he had declined to discuss the question of that country's borders.

Bad news arrived from northern Transylvania, where the regime of Hungarian occupation was rescinding the Romanian agrarian reforms and was expropriating the peasants who had benefited from it—Romanian and Hungarian peasants alike. When I sounded Weizsäcker out about a possible démarche to forestall this despoliation, he turned a deaf ear: this question was too delicate to be raised with Budapest. We were unaccustomed to see such tact and restraint in Nazi diplomacy!

II. 1942

I spent my vacation in Switzerland. My friend Gafencu, who had just settled in Geneva, told me that although he did not want to oppose officially the Antonescu government, he wanted to make it clear that he distanced himself from Romania's current foreign policy. We concurred in our views as to how the war would end, and our personal assessments from Berlin and Moscow, which we compared, yielded the same results. Russia, in his opinion, would play the leading role in Southeastern Europe after the war. He believed that when that took place he would, thanks to his correct past relations with the Kremlin, be the best-qualified person to speak on behalf of Romania with the Moscow government.

FIELD MARSHAL ANTONESCU'S VISIT TO GERMANY

Having returned to my post in Berlin in mid-January, I had to be present at Field Marshal Antonescu's arrival on February 10. Wilhelmstrasse officials had begged me to obtain from him the collar of the Romanian Order of Carol I for Göring, who was of course dying to receive it, and for Ribbentrop, who would die of jealousy if fat Hermann were the only one so honored. What dreams were these men chasing? I tried my damnedest to explain to them that my country's supreme decoration was awarded abroad only to heads of state. Dörnberg replied, "I think that Göring and Ribbentrop carry more weight [one can say that again!] in Europe than the reigning Prince of Liechtenstein, for example!" I tried to explain once again that my monarch could not afford to make any exceptions. But will Antonescu be willing and able to resist the pressure?

A bombshell had just landed, figuratively speaking, for in the literal sense there were many more such explosions: Singapore had fallen. This news did not delight the Germans at all, and, most astonishingly, it even cast a pall over the meetings between the Führer and the Conducător. The vexation went beyond the petty jealousy at seeing an ally, whom one used to disdain a bit, achieve swift, dazzling victories. It was even more than resentment at seeing the Japanese, who had propelled America into the war instead of keeping it on the sidelines, decline to attack the USSR, while selfishly waging their own war. No, it was really the white man injured in his self-esteem. All of Nazi doctrine, all the jumble of prose in *Mein Kampf,* really boiled down to the worshipping of the Aryan race.

What we were witnessing was the yellow race vanquishing the white Anglo-Saxons, which is to say the Germanic race! Through their conquests in Asia, the Japanese were on the brink of acquiring a virtual monopoly over natural rubber production and many other scarce resources. They might become the economic masters of tomorrow. Now, deep down, the Germans pictured more readily how they could hit it off with the Anglo-Saxons than with the yellow race. So Hitler exclaimed: "Here is a piece of news which causes me no pleasure. It has come about too quickly, from the viewpoint of the white race's prestige. And to think that all this could easily have been avoided! The British could have kept their empire intact, if only they had not turned down my peace proposal!" It appeared that the fall of Singapore brought joy to no one, save the Japanese.

In his long private meetings with Hitler, Antonescu handed him a memorandum, which he had read to me—a fairly courageous memorandum, though not a very subtle one. He wanted to learn what military contributions his neighbors would make before determining his own, for he needed his troops not just to retake Bessarabia and northern Bukovina but also to recover the other lost provinces. If need be, he would have to "fight against other countries" than the Soviet Union. Orally, he also complained about the economic plunder to which Romania was subjected and about the extortionist network of German representatives, generals, and crooked businessmen. High-ranking Germans had purchased 400,000 meters of cloth in a single Romanian factory with lei notes issued by the National Bank of Romania and put at the disposal of the occupying forces.

Ribbentrop was cutting a deplorable figure, as usual. He probably thought he was speaking to children, so he poured out a lot of bombast and made ridiculous predictions to his Romanian table companions: a decisive and final German victory was sure to take place in

1942 (previously he had announced it for 1941); Britain, after losing its colonial empire, would become an American dominion, and so on and so on. He alleged he offered Hitler's friendship to Daladier in 1935, yet Daladier did not have the courage to accept it and said to him, "I like you, but I can't do that: they would lynch me in Paris."

A brief visit to Göring's Karinhall. Antonescu's arrival was a bit of a flop. The Romanian field marshal's train carriage stopped beyond the red carpet on which stood Göring with his field marshal's staff in hand. He started shouting, "Zurück, zurück!"[1] The train had to go backward and forward several times in order to get Antonescu and Göring aligned nose-to-nose. There was quite a bit of suppressed giggling, especially among the Romanians.

Karinhall was a Nero-like dream concealed under the modest appearances of a Swedish castle. Inside, however, what profusion of treasures: marvelous eighteenth-century Gobelin or royal Aubusson wall hangings depicting stag hunts, Flemish tapestries from Brussels depicting lion fights, enamels from Limoges (stolen, it was said, from the Rothschild townhouse on rue Saint-Florentin), Roman sarcophagi, columns, marble tables, massive chairs gilded like thrones, statues and bronzes from antiquity, enormous rock crystals, carpets from the Far East or the Savonnerie, paintings by Rubens, van Goyen, Watteau, and Rembrandt. The master of the house wore matchless emerald rings and, alone among all his guests, drank beer from a huge goblet of the same gold as the candelabra on the table, also studded with emeralds. His taste in art was that of a Roman gladiator: he liked objects that glittered brightly and whose appearance was *kolossal.*

At the end of these talks, Antonescu looked tired and discouraged. Neither Hitler, nor Göring, nor Ribbentrop had left him with the slightest hope that the injustice of the Transylvanian settlement would be redressed. He had even been made to understand—in confirmation of the line I suspected the Germans were preparing to take—that the majority of the Transylvanian population was basically composed of Saxons!

I had one last meeting with my country's head of government before he left. I disclosed my fears to him and told him that it would be in his interest to keep an intact army within the country, instead of letting it exhaust itself uselessly on the Russian steppes, while new tasks may await us tomorrow. But the soldier in Antonescu focused on a single goal: to help his ally until the end, for he could see no salvation were the Soviets to take control of Southeastern Europe.

[1]"Back, back!"

Several days later, on February 19, worried by Antonescu's attitude, I sent my government a report in which I advocated:

1. Reducing to a minimum the number of troops on the Russian front, so as to keep the bulk of forces within the country, where they would doubtless have another mission to fulfill in the future.
2. Given present circumstances, espousing a policy of détente toward Bulgaria.
3. Taking a conciliatory attitude, through friendly gestures and declarations, toward the Anglo-American powers, for whom Romanian public opinion universally displayed sentiments of admiration and attachment.

Deputy Prime Minister Mihai ("Ică") Antonescu replied on March 10 with an incensed note. He began by chiding me for "having felt obligated to offer the government certain suggestions relating to the military and diplomatic guidance of the state," an area under the sole purview of "the Foreign Ministry and Field Marshal Antonescu." He proceeded to express surprise over the nature of my proposals; then, mindful of the future's uncertainty, he ended by endorsing my opinion. All that was couched in a jumble of winding phrases, purple prose, and contradictory thoughts, such as this: "Of course I do not remain insensitive to your point of view and I do not think that it was at all ill-considered of you to have shared it with us"—which flatly contradicted the beginning of the note.

On my return to Berlin, I replied as follows, on March 20: "Conscious of the high responsibility vested in my post, and without disputing that it is up to the prime minister and his foreign minister to define our policies, I consider that a foreign envoy of our country is duty-bound not only to send information home but also to draw conclusions about the diplomatic measures that ought to be taken."

I added that, in any case, reticent behavior "was not the understanding I had of my responsibilities as envoy" and that I was "not prepared to jettison my understanding of the job." The government could have drawn its conclusions from this reply and recalled me. That would have fulfilled my fondest wishes. Unfortunately, that did not take place. Aware of the commotion that my departure would cause, it backed down and, on April 5, on the eve of Easter, it sent me a syrupy telegram full of good wishes and thanks for my "fruitful cooperation."

✧ ✧ ✧

I received instructions to apprise Ribbentrop of Hungary's military preparations. These were evidently aimed against southern Transylvania, and a prolonged visit to Sofia by the Hungarian military chief of staff rendered that intent even clearer. These schemes were accompanied by a whole set of unspeakable actions: the wife of my colleague in Budapest, Mrs. Filotti, was verbally abused by a Hungarian cabinet member at the very table of the German envoy in Budapest; the widow of the Transylvanian poet Octavian Goga was insulted by a Hungarian officer and was threatened with the confiscation of her property in Cincea, which included her husband's grave. The Magyar authorities were beginning to suppress the autonomy of the Romanian Church in northern Transylvania. As frosty as ever, Ribbentrop stated that Germany would oppose any armed conflict between countries of Southeastern Europe, yet he offered us no concrete guarantee.

✧ ✧ ✧

There was talk of an Anglo-American landing in Norway, in hope of a linkup with Soviet troops, via Finland. On his return from Stockholm, my Swedish colleague Richert had apparently handed Ribbentrop a diplomatic note confirming Sweden's staunch decision to defend militarily its neutrality against anyone who infringed it. This declaration brought about a détente between Stockholm and Berlin.

The Riom trial,[2] or rather the fashion in which it was proceeding, proved very irritating to the Germans. They had hoped that France itself would be brought to trial and that it would issue a solemn "mea culpa," in which it would disown its entire past history, its whole foreign policy from Cardinal Richelieu to Paul Reynaud, from the Treaty of Westphalia to that of Versailles. Instead, the indictment targeted military unreadiness. The charge brought against the successive governments of the Third Republic was not that they caused the war but that they lost it. And then there were displays of oratory in which Léon Blum and Daladier won new laurels. Relations between Vichy and Berlin suffered as a consequence.

Meanwhile, British warplanes destroyed the Renault factories in Billancourt, which were working for Germany. King Boris arrived in Germany, and that alarmed our Turkish friends. Rumors circulated about Soviet troop landings in Varna and Burgas.

---

[2]Trial of politicians and generals by the Vichy government for having brought France into World War II. The proceedings were suspended in November 1942.

Militarily speaking, time was being marked and one sensed that a great summer offensive would once again be launched. On the eve of such an announcement, it was being whispered again around Wilhelmstrasse that a separate peace arrangement would be welcome news. A separate peace with whom? With the British, if they were willing. Otherwise, with the Russians, to whom "gentle conditions" would be offered.

Himmler was tightening his grip over Germany: having supplanted Göring, he was steadily becoming the real master of the country.

Mussolini and Ciano visited the *Führerhauptquartier* at the end of April. The Duce insisted that the emphasis should be placed on Africa rather than on Russia during the next great offensives.

CONVERSATIONS IN BUCHAREST AND UNFOLDING EVENTS

Short stay in Bucharest, where, on May 11, I once again informed Mihai Antonescu of my desire to leave Berlin. He told me that he was aware of that: "I know you have accepted that assignment as a personal sacrifice for our country. Everyone is grateful to you, and once we find someone of great enough ability to replace you, we will grant your request. But be patient a while longer. Besides, whom would you see in your place?"

I gave a whole list of names—colleagues, politicians, generals. Not one of them suited him. "Wait a while longer, give us the time to find the right person. I beg you not to rush things! Trust me. And, above all, do not speak about this to the field marshal: leave it to me!" Etc., etc.

Two days later, Field Marshal Antonescu imparted to me his certainty that the Germans would be victorious. I let him know my doubts on that score, shared by the impartial witnesses whom I often met in Switzerland. Would it not be wise to entertain the hypothesis of a German defeat? "It is of no use," he answered prophetically, "for if Germany is defeated, the victors in our parts will not be the Anglo-Americans but the Soviets. After that, you don't have to cudgel your brains: the great Communist steamroller will quickly flatten and demolish our European Southeast!" He complained that "all our upper class is pro-British" and he gave me a side glance. The peasants, though, were well aware of the storm that was rising in the east, he said.

✧ ✧ ✧

June 3–7. Vienna, to attend the concert given in honor of our maimed soldiers [being treated in a specialized German hospital]. Our best musicians (Grigoraş Dinicu, Munteanu, etc.). It was pitiful to see our wounded. General Creţoi had lost his left arm, several second lieutenants—mere boys—had lost their right arms. Three officers had been blinded, but smiled broadly when they heard our Romanian songs. It was really shattering.

Luncheon hosted by Baldur von Schirach in the hall of the Vienna Congress. Shamelessly, he pointed out the spot where Dollfuss had been murdered ("where we now drink black coffee!") and, with the mirth of a primitive man, he mocked Schuschnigg. Sztojáy, the Hungarian envoy, laughed and applauded, but became silent when he met my unsmiling and contemptuous gaze.

In the evening, dinner given by the garrison's commander in honor of our wounded Romanian officers. We were informed of the death from his wounds of the murderer Heydrich, the butcher of the Czechs.

✧ ✧ ✧

On Wilhelmstrasse, satisfaction was once again felt about relations with Turkey. The recent economic agreement between the two countries offered Turkey a credit of 100 million Reichsmarks for military purchases and underscored concretely the rapprochement between Berlin and Ankara. A Turkish military commission was present in Berlin, but one tried not to talk too much about it. There was also an easing of tensions between Ankara and Sofia, since the Germans had managed to seal a railway agreement for the Svilengrad-Andrianople rail line. "The German government," Woermann told me, "knows that it will be able to rely on the active friendship of Turkey, should the need arise, but since the present situation does not require its intervention, there is no reason to hasten the evolution of its policies." The Turkish ambassador did not keep his satisfaction secret from me. It was difficult to understand why, given existing circumstances, he was recalled to Ankara and replaced by Asikan, a former education minister and close friend of Ismet Inönü. It was speculated that Gerede may have become too pro-German.

Kallay made his first official visit to Hitler as prime minister of Hungary. It was said that he had used that opportunity to ask for the Serbian Banat and for a revision of the border between Subcarpathian Russia and Poland.

The famous Frank, justice minister, governor of Poland, and president of the German Legal Academy, delivered a new series of lectures, no less startling than his previous talks. This time, the Nazi leader was instructing his listeners about future aspects of Europe, "after the victory of the Axis." There would no longer be that democratic scattering of little countries imagined by the League of Nations; it would be replaced by a *Völkerkameradschaft,* a comradeship of peoples, led by Germany, which would leave each nation "its complete sovereignty and independence in regard to culture." But political and military independence would have to be relinquished to the power that would lead the destinies of Europe. In another lecture, he declared that judges, in the future, would also enjoy independence, but not "political independence." German understanding of law would remain the foundation of the European legal order and its executive arm would be the Berlin-Rome Axis. Soon enough, his successor, Thierack, was going to state that judges owed greater obedience to their National-Socialist consciences than to the legal code. What ever became of the miller of Sans-Souci?

✧ ✧ ✧

Vacation in Sinaia. I took the opportunity once again to ask Mihai Antonescu to find a replacement for me. I told him how sick I was of my post. The Germans were indifferent to the fate of the Romanians in northern Transylvania and we gave in to them on all points. He promised to relieve me soon.

OASIS: AN ANACHRONISTIC PRINCELY WEDDING

An oasis in the moral desert of contemporary Germany: a princely wedding in Sigmaringen, during the waning days of August 1942. I was there to represent my sovereign, also a member of that house of Catholic Hohenzollerns, who for more than a thousand years have resided near the source of the Danube. The nuptials united the young Princess Maria-Adelgunde, second daughter of Prince Friedrich von Hohenzollern (head of the family) and his wife, Margarete (daughter of the last king of Saxony), to the equally young Konstantin of Bavaria (son of Prince Adalbert and a Countess Seefried). It was a belated vision of pre-1914 Europe. In addition to all the family members, the following persons gathered in the medieval castle: former Queen Augusta of Portugal (widow of Manuel II, presently married to a Count Douglas, and sister of the lord of the castle), the Margrave of Meissen (quasi king of Saxony), and Prince Ludwig Ferdinand of Prussia (quasi Kronprinz), with their respective wives. Also the charming countenances of old ladies who looked as though they had just stepped out of eighteenth-century sedan chairs: the Princesses Friedrich and Wilhelm of Hohenzollern (the former née Thurn und Taxis, the latter née Wittelsbach) and Princess Johann Georg of Saxony (née Bourbon-Sicilies). Resplendent pre-1914 military uniforms, neck chains and grand sashes of decorations abolished long ago, old titles still recorded only in the *Almanach de Gotha,* speeches as if from one sovereign to another, uttered in fact by ghosts. It was Sleeping Beauty's castle, roused by a magic wand from its centuries-long lethargy. Court procession from the castle to the church, over a red carpet that wound through the streets of the peaceful sleepy town. I offered my arm to Princess Albert von Hohenzollern, the bride's aunt. The Prince of Hohenzollern had just conferred on me the first class cross of his House's order. (The occasion would have been more solemn had he not surprised me in shirtsleeves as I was dressing up.) He begged me not to speak about the matter, for Hitler had forbidden him to bestow decorations. "And that," he told me, "even though my great-grandfather, in ceding his principality to Prussia, expressly retained that specific right!" How it all preserved an aura of the ancien régime and its court etiquette! It enabled us to forget for a moment the hideous swastikas and ash-colored uniforms.

After the wedding, which lasted three days as in old fairy tales, I took Ludwig Ferdinand and Kyra of Prussia to visit Burg Hohenzollern, birthplace of their family, an unfortunate fake Gothic reconstruction of the 1860s, then we spent twenty-four hours in Langenstein Castle, home of former Queen Augusta of Portugal and her current morganatic spouse, Count Douglas. It was a beautiful sixteenth-century manor that had remained unchanged, though the estate was a model of agricultural efficiency. The beehives were weighed each day to see how much honey the bees had produced! We were offered port wine of 1810 vintage, the oldest that I ever drank in my life.

DIFFICULT DEALINGS WITH THE GERMANS

The oasis was left behind. I returned to Berlin's heavy and anguishing atmosphere. The usually unctuous Weizsäcker, backed up by Erdmannsdorf, more or less blew his stack at me because the brochures that our propaganda ministry had prepared for a Romanian ethnographic exhibit on tour in several German cities contained truths such as:

"Transylvania is the cradle of the Romanian nation" and "Romanians are struggling to recover their natural frontiers."

Since his reproaches and his tone seemed to me out of place and smacked of a boor who thought he was allowed to lord it over "little countries," I got ticked off, cut him short, and told him I would inform my government about his tirade. I would be interested to see, I added, whether his bosses would approve of it, at a time when Romanian soldiers—including those who came from Transylvania—were shedding their blood on battlefields. These words produced the effect of a cold shower on the old secretary of state: realizing that a complaint by Ion Antonescu to Hitler would unquestionably entail a sharp reprimand from his irascible Führer, he looked with distress at his colleague, sweetened his tune, and congratulated me for the glorious military actions of Romania. But I paid no attention to this belated eulogy of our troops and departed.

The incident reached Ribbentrop's ears, and he beseeched Mihai Antonescu to let me know that "Weizsäcker only wanted to mention this question in passing and regrets that you have interpreted it otherwise and found his tone out of place." I should say, out of fairness to old Weizsäcker, that he had been worked up by his close friend Sztojáy, the Hungarian envoy, who was to end his life tragically before a firing squad. Moreover, Weizsäcker's nerves were shot since the death of his son on the Polish front.

But there were other causes of worry for me. The Saxons and Swabians of Transylvania and the Banat were being stirred up. Their youths were in Germany, drafted either into the German army, the SS, or party organizations. They all requested autonomy for the regions from which they came. They demanded "a state within the state." A customs union between Romania and the Reich was demanded by their leader, Andreas Schmidt, a Nazi through and through, and even by Rudolf Brandsch, one of their older politicians, a former Romanian undersecretary of state who benefited from a hefty subsidy from the Romanian government. That boded well for the future, were the Germans to win the war! I warned my government about what was being schemed, and I never missed an opportunity in Berlin to explain how unfeasible such fantasies were.

A SEPARATE GERMAN PEACE WITH RUSSIA?

At the end of September, Hitler and Ribbentrop prophesied that Stalingrad would fall shortly. But very soon the German people realized that nothing of the kind would happen. This first defeat, this first fiasco, would set in motion the movement that came to be called "Underground Germany." It also prompted the Germans to begin in Stockholm secret negotiations with the USSR toward making a separate peace.

Rosenberg, Ritter, and Schulenburg independently confided to me that, once its military objectives in the east had been attained, the Reich would see no drawback in reaching a separate peace with Stalin, who was himself dissatisfied with the insufficient assistance provided to him by his allies. That explained the absence of invectives against the USSR in recent speeches by Hitler, Göring, Ribbentrop, and Goebbels, who all confined themselves to attacking the Anglo-American powers. Göring had said, "Roosevelt, Churchill, and Stalin: of the three it is Stalin who is the superior one." At a luncheon in our legation, Ambassador Ritter, the Reich's "economic czar," who always dogged Hitler's heels and dwelt in his headquarters, did not hesitate to make the following remark, before all the guests: "It is public knowledge that Hitler and Stalin have the highest regard for each other." What a look was to be seen on the face of my Portuguese colleague, Count Tovar, who whispered to me, "In other words, is he announcing to us a separate peace?" Moreover, Stalin had removed the political commissars from his army, as if to please the Germans. Was it not plausible that von Papen was secretly negotiating in Ankara on the following basis: surrender of the Ukraine and the Caucasus, economic collaboration? General Shaposhnikov had supposedly been given command of the army in order to sign an armistice.

Rosenberg seemed to be living in the clouds. During a dinner at the Italian embassy, he outlined to the other guests his plans for a future "colonization" of Russia: Dutchmen would be relocated in the Wolin region, Danes in the Ukraine, etc., etc. "Russia will become a new Germany." Science fiction worthy of a bad Jules Verne novel. My wife cut in to ask whether he really thought one could turn a European country with a white population into a colony. Rosenberg answered yes, and cited as examples the ancient Romans who colonized Gaul and the Germans relocated in Transylvania, the Banat, and Bessarabia. And what about the Russian people, so great in numbers, she asked? Would they accept being permanently ruled by Germans? What madness, and how appropriate for a man who imagined he could found a new religion in the middle of the twentieth century.

Serious German-Danish tensions. Among occupied countries, Denmark had enjoyed a favored status. Now Hitler wanted to tighten the screws, at least so as to draw a greater economic contribution. To a long, effusive telegram of birthday greetings that Hitler had sent him, the king had responded too laconically, "Best thanks. Christian R." Hitler seized this as a pretext to recall Reuthe-Fink, his envoy in Copenhagen, and also General Lütke, commander of the occupying troops—both were accused of limpness. He demanded the departure of Mohr, the Danish envoy in Berlin. Simultaneously an ultimatum of sorts was sent to the Scavenius government in order to secure important economic concessions, a huge increase in Danish exports to Germany (made available on credit, of course), and the collaboration of Danish police agencies with the SS in suppressing acts of sabotage. On the horizon one could already make out what further demands would follow: arming the Danish commercial fleet for use against Britain, Denmark's entry into war against the USSR, perhaps even integration of the kingdom of Christian X into an expanded German Reich!

END OF MY MISSION

The Romanian government was still disinclined to grant my request and relieve me of my duties as head of the Berlin legation. An incident with the German general staff provoked by Mihai Antonescu, in which he had tried to shield himself by invoking my name, gave me the opportunity to send my official written resignation to the king and Field Marshal Antonescu. But an appeal was once again made to my patriotic feelings and my duty to stick to my post in time of war. Nevertheless, I was determined that, after my next trip to Bucharest, regardless of the government's reaction to my decision, I would not continue my assignment in Germany.

Given that decision, I put my affairs in order; in a report to Bucharest I explained where matters stood. I reviewed Germany's difficulties as the fourth winter of war loomed ahead. Understandably, subversive currents were swelling. The daily hardships and anxieties already felt by the population several years before the war had been tolerable while military victories had allowed people to hope that a swift and favorable end of hostilities might be around the corner. Now, however, the difficulties and setbacks of the African campaign had made this hope more distant and lowered public morale. What a difference there was between the mood a year and a half earlier, when I took up my appointment, and what I saw around me as I prepared to leave!

It was not, precisely speaking, outright defeatism. Who would dare show it? Such an avowal would lead to certain death, preceded to be sure by grisly tortures. A gruesome joke was making the rounds: a Berliner was asked whether he believed in Germany's final victory. He replied, *"Ich habe lieber am Endsieg zu glauben als ohne Kopf herumzulaufen."*[3] No, it was an intangible feeling, an indefinite and vague malaise that floated about. It was *Kriegsmüdigkeit*[4]—a term coined on the pattern of *Schneemüdigkeit,* that nagging weariness of snow that one feels at the end of winter. Women separated from their husbands for over three years, mothers who lost, one by one, all their sons—it was they who, without a doubt, first sowed that psychosis of despair in drab, gray, indefinite silence.

I wrote in a report dated November 9: "There is no longer a single soul in Germany who believes that Britain and the United States will collapse. It is the Germans' illusions that have collapsed, one after the other: 'Soviet disorganization,' 'Russia's rapid fragmentation,' 'the spread of the National-Socialist system throughout all countries,' 'the brotherly collaboration of European peoples under the swastika's protection,' 'total control of the sky, which rules out bombing raids on German cities,' etc. Now, in North Africa, the American factor is added onto the scales. Doubts begin to emerge as to the future attitude of Germany's allies, who wish to pull free while there is still time."

What were they coming up with to stem the tide of discouragement? A speech by the Führer, on November 8, in the traditional Löwenbräukeller of Munich, with the party's old guard in attendance. What did he say? Well, he had softened his tune. Gone were those aggressive expressions he so loved, such as: *vollkommene Zerschlagung der Feindes,*[5] *Vernichtung unserer Gegner,*[6] or *Zerschmetterung der Plutokratien.*[7] Hitler traded them all in for a more concise declaration that was also more explicit: *"Ich kapituliere nicht."*[8] In reference to the new turn of events in North Africa, he added that "in order to redress the situation, everything will be done that is needed and feasible." These statements were interpreted and discussed by the people. It might have seemed encouraging that he vowed to do everything possible to resolve difficulties and that he did not intend to surrender.

Concerning Europe's alleged spirit of solidarity with Hitler, I pointed out that "it has never existed so far, and neither the oppression of entire nations nor the arbitrary redrawing of borders is likely to bring it about." In my diary I noted: "Today, November 9, 1942, Germany has

---

[3]"I would rather believe in final victory than run around without my head."
[4]War fatigue.
[5]Total destruction of the enemy.
[6]Annihilation of our foes.
[7]Smashing apart of the plutocracies.
[8]"I will not surrender."

unquestionably lost World War II. Fateful justice triumphs, as always. What will Romania do? Our situation is critical. Will divine providence give us the wisdom and courage needed to act decisively?"

The following day I cabled: "The military situation in North Africa is taking the dimension of a major military disaster for the Germans and Italians. Once in control of Africa, the Anglo-American troops will be able to open a second front in Europe."

On November 30, I sent my government the following report concerning the state of mind in Germany: "I would be neglecting my basic duty, which is to inform the government with utterly disinterested frankness, if I did not draw your attention to the profound impact of military developments in Africa and on the eastern front on German public opinion. Earlier disillusionment about the length of the war, Britain's tenacity, and enemy bombing raids—all those disappointments are now fatally increased for the German people by new, cruel doubts about their Italian ally's solidarity 'to the final hour,' the Wehrmacht's invincible might, and the unerring foresight of their leaders.

"In all the countries of the world, public opinion grants the government's declarations a certain authority, but no mystical and prophetic power. In the Third Reich, however, pronouncements handed down from the state's highest sphere were until now taken as true oracles, open to neither commentary nor discussion, and incapable of containing the slightest mistake, even on small details. Should one or another of these prophecies not come to pass, in its entirety and on the date specified, then faith itself begins to totter.

"Last year, on March 27, Ribbentrop assured his guests, in the toast he made at the banquet for Matsuoka, that the German final victory would occur before the end of 1941. On September 27 of that same year he stated his conviction that Stalingrad would soon fall. On October 1, Hitler himself asserted, 'The Germans will take Stalingrad, it is I who tell you so.' Finally, on October 5, Field Marshal Rommel swore that he would never relinquish the positions he had won in Egypt. Any other nation would have understood that all these utterances expressed projects, hopes, or personal convictions—but not prophecies. However, the German nation thought that it was listening to the verdict of history, and it is simply astounded that history has failed to comply with the will of those who spelled out that verdict.

"There is something tragic in the German character, a combination of contradictory traits—lyricism and cruelty, assertiveness and inhibition (the famous *Hemmungen*)—that afflict its inner life and sap its seeming self-confidence. The man in the street has never been excessively optimistic even in times of spectacular victories; one may recall the famous quip, *Wir siegen uns zu Tode.*[9] All the more reason to feel depressed in the current phase of the world war. If he ever deluded himself into dreaming that this huge conflagration would end favorably, that dream is surely dispelled by now. If he goes one step farther, he will gradually distance himself from the party structures. On the other hand, he likes to steep himself again in army traditions: 'We have been ruled by civilians,' a German said to me, 'because our heroes of 1914–1918 disappeared and we had no one around whom to gather; but now we have heroes once again.' The regime of repression, surveillance, and swift punishment under which Germany now lives keeps the evolution of public consciousness under wraps. Nevertheless, opinions are beginning to be more boldly expressed, party emblems are less frequently displayed, partisan zeal is tending to abate."

On December 3, as a final item in the inventory that I was drawing up, I sent my government a report on the Transylvanian question in which I asserted, on the basis of a whole series of arguments and proofs, that the Nazi regime firmly intended to turn this province into an autonomous state ruled by the Saxons. One of the conclusions I reached was that only the Atlantic Charter, only the political principles defended by the Allies, could help us to reintegrate Transylvania fully and permanently within the Romanian state. Another conclusion: do not give the Germans the impression that Romania might be very interested in things to the east, for that would encourage them to ask us at once for concessions on the western flank.

My last meeting with Ribbentrop left me with a deplorable memory of him. Pale and sweating, he gave me a long soliloquy describing Germany's favorable report card up to this day. In every area he perceived victories—or rather, he endeavored to make me perceive them. Military defeats were only temporary difficulties. I brought up objections: America's impressive rate of military goods production, the unrest in the Balkans, the growth of the Communist movement throughout Europe. Gliding past these thorny issues, he asserted *"Dieser Krieg ist nicht zu verlieren!"*[10] He complained about Maniu and Romanian political circles that anticipated an Anglo-American victory without discerning the Russian peril. I replied that the stance taken by the Axis on the question of Transylvania, whose Romanian population was subjected to Magyar oppression, was largely

[9] We triumph ourselves to death.

[10] "This war is not one to be lost!"

what rendered our politicians unresponsive to Axis policies and made Iuliu Maniu a very popular historical figure—a great Romanian, who was also a great Transylvanian. He was the living symbol of that province, for whose liberation he had fought before 1914. He was looking for the political arrangement that was most likely to bring back to us all of Transylvania. Ribbentrop hastened to change the subject, then I left and never saw him again.

Subsequently, I sent Mihai Antonescu a letter, dated December 15, in which, for the fifth time, I tendered my resignation, and I insisted that he submit it to the king. After more hesitations, it was finally accepted, but I was asked to remain in my post until a successor could be appointed.

III. 1943

END OF MY MISSION (CONT.)

At a final dinner in Potsdam (January 19), at the house of Princess Feodora von Schaumburg-Lippe, née Princess of Denmark, Ambassador von Hassell, who was to meet a tragic end, confided to me in private that he was convinced the Allies would never sign a peace with Hitler and that "National-Socialism should vanish while there is still time." In such a scenario, he foresaw the creation of a military government, headed either by Field Marshal von Witzleben or by Field Marshal von Falkenhausen, neither of whom had ever been compromised by dealings with the ruling party. It would, however, be a "nationalist" government, which consequently would not accept the partition or occupation of Germany. If such a humiliation and destruction of the country were absolutely insisted on, the country would sink into communism, which would not be in the Anglo-Americans' interest.

Whereas Paul Schmidt, head of the Wilhelmstrasse's press service, announced that Churchill was on his way to Washington, we learned on January 27 that he was in fact, and had been for ten days, with Roosevelt, de Gaulle, and Giraud in Casablanca, where the Allies issued their famous demand for the unconditional surrender of Germany, Italy, and Japan. I felt this was somewhat clumsy, for if they wanted to win over public opinion in Italy and Germany, they should have left the door ajar for some hope.

February 4. I arrived in Bucharest, and went to see Secretary-General Davidescu at the Ministry. He told me that after at first denying in writing my last request to be released from my posting in Berlin, Mihai Antonescu had withdrawn his opposition, saying, "You cannot keep someone by force in such a post." But a successor "worthy of such a predecessor" was still being sought, kindly added Davidescu. He feared violent German reactions to our modest attempts to assert our economic, diplomatic, or political independence (such as the refusal to break relations with Chile, or our refusal to take any measures against Maniu, as demanded by Ribbentrop).

February 6. A long meeting with Mihai Antonescu, who was surprisingly friendly. He began by thanking me for my work in Berlin: "I realize that your mission there constitutes for you a sacrifice made out of patriotism. I know your views and I understand how painful this sacrifice is. I also can imagine what sacrifice it is for Mrs. Bossy to live in Berlin under present circumstances, separated from your children and with her great worry about her brother, missing in action on the eastern front. I had meant to send her a cable; please tell her how much I think of her sadness, and give her my respectful regards. I therefore fully agree that you be relieved, as you have requested, of your mission as envoy of Romania in Berlin."

[After discussing possible replacements in Berlin, I told him] I wanted to turn to political issues. Although often interrupted, I told him about the military and political situation in Germany, about some emerging trends against the party and the SS and in favor of the army, which was seen as a possible political standby in the future. I disclosed to him the plans that were being hatched for a future transition government that could eventually treat with the Allies. I would not be astonished, I said, if Ciano's departure [from the Ministry of Foreign Affairs] represented a division of roles in Italy: Mussolini pursuing the war *usque ad finem,* while his son-in-law kept from now on his distance so as to be able to make certain contacts and, at the decisive hour, to take the succession in order to negotiate with the Anglo-Americans (were these willing to talk with him, which I doubted). After I described the atmosphere in Germany, where no one still believed in victory and the fear of tomorrow was growing, Mihai Antonescu asked me if I thought that, in case of Germany's defeat, the Anglo-Americans would be willing to negotiate with a government led by Göring. I answered "no": after the call for unconditional surrender, it was crystal clear in my view that the total elimination of all totalitarian regimes was sought, and that as a result there would be no negotiation with any representative of the National-Socialist regime.

I asked in turn whether our government was giving thought to such a contingency, whether it had made contacts, and whether we were limiting our efforts on the eastern front—efforts that had gone beyond the call of loyalty—so as to preserve in the country an army we absolutely needed, not only against the Hungarians but also so as to count for something in the eyes of the Anglo-Americans, especially if they were thinking of establishing, later on, centers of resistance against Bolshevik expansion. Mihai Antonescu replied that he had some contacts through neutral countries, such as Switzerland and Portugal. It was also for that end that he wanted to use our foremost diplomats, with long-established and valuable relationships, giving them "coordinating" missions that would justify their presence abroad and give them greater freedom of action than that of the accredited envoys. The first name to come to his mind for such a mission had been mine. He would also have recourse to Cretzianu, with whom he had resumed relations. With regard to our operations on the eastern front, they had been excessive, but that was what the field marshal wanted. Personally, Mihai Antonescu had been against our participation in the war with Russia, and especially on such a scale. I reminded him that when I had set forth similar views in a top-secret report, he had rejected them in a most unpleasant way. He said I had been right and confessed that he had shared my views, but had replied to me as he did by order of the field marshal. (This explanation did not satisfy me. In his place, I would not have signed a paper stating the opposite of my beliefs. Or at least I would not dissociate myself now—rather inelegantly—from the one whose views I had adopted.) From now on, he assured me, we would take all necessary measures to have a strong army in our country. By summer, we will have a new army of 500,000 men, albeit without much air support and anti-aircraft or anti-tank artillery.

February 8. Alexander Cretzianu told me how the hatchet had been buried between him and Mihai ("Ică") Antonescu. Secretary-General Davidescu had asked Cretzianu to come see him, and Ică had "just happened" to come by. Ică told Cretzianu that he had always been fond of him and that if he had sent him such a "stern" letter, it was by order of Field Marshal Antonescu (again that leitmotiv). He then described at length his diplomatic activities, wanting to justify himself as if he were asking Cretzianu to defend him in front of the Allies! All this because he wanted some people (Savel Rădulescu, Al. Cretzianu, etc.) to go abroad to defend the country's interests . . . and to save his skin.

I took the opportunity to ask Cretzianu why, knowing my feelings, he had not tried to save me from being posted to Berlin. He said that after the crushing of the Iron Guard rebellion, Field Marshal Antonescu had refused to appoint to Berlin and Rome "outsiders" (who would try to undermine him in order to push themselves forward), and had asked who were our best heads of mission; Cretzianu had mentioned Grigorcea and me. He believed Field Marshal Antonescu must have passed these names on to the Germans, who then made inquiries into our preceding assignments. It is likely that the appraisal given by Mackensen, with whom I had been three times in the same posting, must have done me a "disservice" because, faced with his laudatory comments about me, Antonescu did not hesitate to choose me for Berlin.

February 9. Field Marshal Antonescu received me at the Presidency of the Council. Since Mihai Antonescu had asked me insistently not to mention my desire to leave Berlin (for he would seek "the appropriate moment and a favorable disposition" to settle the matter), the conversation was limited to political topics. He asked for my views. I told him that I felt duty-bound to speak frankly, without holding anything back: there was no longer anyone in Germany who still believed in a final worldwide victory. Even the number of those who would wish it was falling, for fear of perpetuating the National-Socialist regime. To be sure, there still were some, especially in official circles, who spoke with conviction of a crushing victory over the Bolsheviks in an offensive that, forgoing territorial acquisitions, would be aimed at annihilating this summer the Soviet armed might. But, I stressed, their number seemed to be dwindling. Public opinion was defeatist, discouraged. There was almost panic. Famine, however, had been kept at bay. Everybody ate poorly and little—but sufficiently. And there was a truly exemplary fairness in the allocation of food. Even Mrs. Meissner (the wife of the head of Hitler's Chancellery) had asked my wife if she could give her some butter coupons,[1] proof that no one was privileged. Therefore, the facts that food was available in the strictly necessary amounts, that the black market had almost completely disappeared, and that social equality had been entrenched—as well as the unforgiving Gestapo surveillance—did not permit the illusion of an imminent revolution. But thought was given to future modes of government that would allow talks with the enemy, who was becoming the victor. The idea of a military transition government was being aired.

Field Marshal Antonescu heard me out in silence. After that, he told me that my perceptions did not tally with reality because, like all diplo-

[1]Foreign missions had a larger allocaton of rationing coupons, and could also obtain rationed goods from abroad.

mats, I was misled by the aristocratic and cosmopolitan milieu in which I lived. "And foreign diplomats in Bucharest [he went on] are similarly mistaken about the atmosphere in Romania. Seeing only ladies from our upper class and moving only in anglophile circles, they imagine that this country is pro-British, while in fact the people follow me one hundred percent. That is the difference between the regime of Pétain—who is not followed by the French and has remained isolated—and my regime. The proof: in Carol II's time you could see sentries everywhere, and all institutions were guarded by the army, a sign of general uncertainty. Now, everybody moves around freely and unguarded."

Odd statement, since in those days one could see more military guards than ever. That same day, in order to get to the field marshal, I had gone through I don't know how many checkpoints, and had had to state my name and position to I don't know how many successive sentries, almost ready to search me.

Returning to his topic, Field Marshal Antonescu told me: "I have many officers in Germany, buying military equipment. They visit factories and workshops, not fashionable salons. All report to me that the workers are disciplined, enthusiastic, and convinced of Germany's final victory. This is the true atmosphere in Germany, and it is on it that I base my plans. And then, you are not aware of the secret arms that Hitler showed me during our last meeting, nor of his war plans, nor of the host of soldiers he will throw upon the Russians this summer. There is no doubt whatsoever that the German summer offensive will crush the Russian army."

He told me there had been some quite serious incidents between German troops and ours, but that Hitler had promised to issue the required orders to his officers to punish severely any lack of comradeship toward the Romanians. At one point he told me, "You know, even in England and America we are not viewed badly." As for the strategy of Hitler—"who is not a professional soldier"—he had some reservations: serious mistakes had been made both in evaluating the opposing forces and in establishing too distant objectives for the offensive. With regard to Transylvania, he had told Hitler: "I will recover it, and without your help, for if a country of sixteen and a half million inhabitants is not able to free one and a half million brothers oppressed by a smaller country, it does not deserve to live."

February 21. I lunched with Davidescu (secretary-general of the Ministry of Foreign Affairs) at Capşa. He proposed that I be transferred from Berlin to Stockholm. I answered that once I was freed from my present posting, I would much prefer not to undertake another foreign mission until the end of the war. In any case, family reasons compelled me to stay in Switzerland until fall.

March 4. New meeting with Mihai Antonescu. He told me to be absolutely confident that I would be transferred from Berlin: "We cannot keep you there against your will." But he asked me to remain in Bucharest for a while, because Grigorcea was expected to come from Rome, and if he agreed to be transferred to the Royal Palace—for the time being he still hesitated—it would not be possible to have simultaneous changes in the two capitals of the Axis, so that my transfer would have to be postponed by two months. But it would not be necessary for me to stay in Berlin all that time; I could shuttle to and from Copenhagen, and later go to Switzerland, from where I could ask for a medical leave.

March 8. It is rumored in town that the field marshal and Ică Antonescu are at daggers drawn, and that the latter would want to be a "Darlan less the assassination."

Davidescu told me he had been instructed by Ică to offer me Ankara. I replied that I had to remain in Switzerland until fall, because of my wife's pregnancy. I was also offered the Vatican; I made the same reply as for Stockholm and Ankara.

April 8. Since the issue of my transfer continued to remain in suspense for lack of an able and willing successor, I left to settle in Switzerland, without waiting for my replacement to be appointed.

June 11. A phone call from Berlin informed me that the German government had given its agreement to the appointment of General Gheorghe as Romanian envoy. At last!

June 14. Having now been officially informed of General Gheorghe's appointment as Romanian envoy to Berlin, I left [for Germany and Denmark] to make my farewell calls.

June 18. Arrived in Berlin, I invited Friedl Hohenzollern and his son to lunch; they are leaving for Dresden for the burial of Prince George of Saxony.

In the afternoon, I received the visit of the Baar-Baarenfels couple. He, former vice-chancellor of Austria and my former colleague in Budapest, had spent four years in Dachau along with the young Hohenbergs, the sons of Franz Ferdinand. He recounted to me the atrocities he underwent (exhausting and degrading work—cleaning the latrines—beatings, tortures). He came to envy the street sweeps. Many died during the tortures. Now, he and all the other Austrian notables have been set free. He had even been given a low-level job at I.G. Farben Industrie. But after all he has gone through, he is a spent man. I expressed to him my indignation and revulsion at the treatment he had been subjected to simply because he was an Austrian patriot. I assured him that some day all of this would be paid for in full and more, for God's mill grinds slowly, but exceedingly fine.

June 22. Farewell visits to Erdmannsdorf and Clodius, and to my Slovak, Bulgarian, Turkish, and Swedish colleagues. In the evening, I gave an informal dinner party for the friends we had made here: Countess Bethe von Werthern, Princess Louise of Prussia, Prince and Princess Maxl Schaumburg-Lippe, Princesses Edda and Carmen Wiede, and so forth.

June 24. Farewell calls on my Italian, Danish, and Finnish colleagues, as well as on the new secretary of state von Steengracht, who informed me that the unofficial Romano-Hungarian talks conducted by Mironescu and Bánffy have collapsed. Farewell luncheon hosted by protocol chief and Baroness Dörnberg. In the evening, dinner at Arikan's, Turkey's ambassador, who told me, "Both now and at the peace negotiations, we will work with the Romanians, and for the Romanians."

June 25. Farewell visits to my Swiss, Japanese, and Spanish colleagues. In the afternoon, I invited my staff to tea, to take leave from them. In their name, M. Stănescu gave me a large silver dish engraved with their signatures.

June 26. I continue my series of farewell visits with calls on Meissner (Chancellery of the Reich), Chwalkowski (Czech legation), and Tovar (Portuguese legation). Appalled, Chwalkowski talks to me about the terror unleashed in his country by the Germans. Many of his colleagues in the Ministry of Foreign Affairs have been killed by the Gestapo. Contrary to rumors, Fiša is fortunately not among them. Luncheon with my staff and their wives, hosted in my honor by Stănescu in the former apartment of the Schelihas, where I had spent many pleasant hours but which is filled by a gloomy atmosphere since it was confirmed that poor von Scheliha had been hanged by the Gestapo for "treason." Tea with Feo Schaumburg and Isi Preussen, who give me letters for the Danish sovereigns.

June 27. I leave by car for Copenhagen, accompanied by Cernak, my Slovak colleague in both Germany and Denmark.

June 30. Farewell call on Scavenius, prime minister and minister of foreign affairs. He complains of the precarious economic situation in which Denmark has fallen because of German exactions. Both Germany and its opponents are still very strong, so no end of the war can be expected soon.

July 1. Audience with the Danish sovereigns in their residence of Sorgenfri, close to the capital. Comfortable country house, but with all the court's formalities and ceremonials observed. I handed King Christian X my recall letter. "But why aren't you staying on with us? You should have got rid of the posting to Berlin, but kept on to the one to Copenhagen." I told him that that had been my intention, but that "the diplomat proposes, but his government disposes." He laughed. He inquired about King Michael and Queen Mother Helen. Then about his grandnieces from Berlin, Isi Preussen and Feo Schaumburg, with whom he knew we were friends.

We then turned to politics. He launched into his usual and bitter diatribe against the Germans. I told him how stirring it was to see an entire nation so closely gathered around its king and with such monarchic loyalty. He seemed touched. With moist eyes, he answered: "Yes, my Danes do rather like me. But when one holds the position I hold—and that for thirty-one years!—one must do one's duty. I hope I did mine. At each German encroachment, I slap their wrists: I protest, I remind them of their commitments. But to do so I must stay in Copenhagen. The people insist on seeing me every day. I therefore await impatiently to recover from the injuries I incurred when I was thrown off my horse to return to town."

We noted a certain similarity in the situations of our two countries—but without the proximity of the Soviet Union, I stressed. He believes the war will last two more years. At the end of our talk, which lasted forty minutes, he bestowed on me the grand cross of the order of Danebrog (with collar) "in memory of your too short stay among us, and to remind you of Denmark, a country that suffers just like yours and which, like yours, believes in better days to come."

I then went to see the queen, who questioned me at length about my wife and about her grandnieces, Isi Preussen and Feo Schaumburg. I handed her the letters the latter had entrusted to me, and she asked me to take along parcels and letters for them. When I was leaving, she asked me to give my wife "my very best regards and all my wishes for the expected baby."

Since the Danes were bravely resisting and their underground movement had begun a heroic struggle, the iron fist of the Nazis, shedding its fake velvet glove, was soon to clamp down on the admirable Danish nation and imprison its great king. The Scavenius government would resign a few months later so as not to give the appearance of consenting to this act of violence, and various administrative departments would be run only by secretary-generals.

July 5. Back in Berlin, Feo Schaumburg came to have tea with me. She asked for news from Copenhagen and about the Danish king and queen, whose letters and parcels I gave her. She doesn't dare go there (even were the Germans to give her a return visa), since, as a German princess, she would be ostracized, notwithstanding the fact that she was born princess of Denmark. She longs for a British invasion, which would bring about peace.

July 6. Farewell luncheon hosted in my honor by Steengracht, secretary of state at the Foreign Ministry, at the Adlon. All the bigwigs from Wilhelmstrasse attended, as did my staff from the legation. The de rigueur toasts, much bonhomie. For the last time, I raised the issue of Transylvania. I underscored that the Hencke-Roggieri report plainly states that the majority of the population in the area ceded to Hungary is Romanian. Steengracht admitted this was true but added, "Nevertheless, this problem cannot be broached until the end of the war."

July 7. Dörnberg shows up with two enormous Nymphenburg vases, a parting gift from the German government. He told me that Ribbentrop chose them himself, having two similar ones in his office. At 8 P.M., departure from the Anhalter railway station. Erdmannsdorf, Dörnberg, and other officials from the Ausswertiges Amt see me off, as well as all my staff from the legation. My foreign colleagues were unable to come, being invited for dinner by the nuncio, but they all phoned or wrote me to wish me good-bye.

I finally leave Berlin for good, after two years and three months. Thank God!

13

The End of a Career (1943–1946)

1943

July 8. Happy to be reunited with Senta and the children in Lausanne. I am now being offered Stockholm, which I turn down.

July 14. A great joy for all of us: the birth of our fourth child and second son.

July 25. The fall of the Fascist regime, the fall of Mussolini. The dawn of peace seems to draw closer for Italy.

August 8. Under great pressure to accept being appointed to the Vatican—even though I would find it so painful, and probably useless, to represent a government headed by the Antonescus—I departed for Bucharest, leaving Senta still recuperating.

August 13. Alexander Cretzianu, who is being appointed to Ankara, strongly insisted that I go to the Vatican because our mission is no longer to represent the Antonescu regime but to present to the Anglo-American victors the Romanian case. I replied that, in my view, it would be much more effective if he and I were entrusted not with official missions (which would force us after all to speak in the name of the Antonescu regime), but with an informal one, more favorable to certain contacts.

August 21. Meeting with Mihai Antonescu. Most cordial and friendly. He regrets that I could not be appointed to Berne, but there is need for a man of real ability (and not divorced) for the Vatican, and there is no one else but me!

August 22. Audience and lunch at the Foişor Palace, with the king and queen mother. A friendly and free conversation, in English. They both seemed very worried. I explained to them that I would have considered an informal mission to be more appropriate in today's situation, and to enable me to say what I had to say, than an official one. Both agreed, but Sitta remarked that "Mihai Antonescu is so keen on your going to the Vatican, it won't be possible to change his mind." She would want me to get in touch with Osborne, the British envoy to the Vatican, and she might write him to introduce me. She asked me to tell Osborne what the king's true feelings are, and to urge him to explain to London that the king is a prisoner but that, at the useful moment (but not before) he would make the expected move. A hasty move would lead to the country's occupation by the Germans and the king's fleeing abroad. The idea of a flight abroad seems to obsess the queen and her son. I told them that the king should have recourse to flight only as a last resort. He should try to remain in place, like the kings of Belgium and Denmark, for one knows when a dynasty leaves, but no one knows when it will come back.

August 25. Dr. Costinescu believes I should go to the Vatican, for it is a posting from which one can get in touch with the Anglo-Americans. There, I should not speak in the name of the government, but only in that of the king and of the Romanian people. I would be introduced to Osborne by Maniu and Dinu Brătianu, who have direct contacts with London. He then appointed me as a representative of the Romanian Red Cross to the International Red Cross, so that I might travel even when the Allies occupy Rome.

Vişoianu, on the other hand, believes it would be preferable for Cretzianu and me not to accept official missions, since as representatives of the government, the Anglo-Americans would give us less credence than were we entrusted with unofficial missions.

August 26. Meeting with Mihai Antonescu. "Time is pressing," he said, "and we must make a decision regarding the Vatican. Have you given it thought? I have the impression you have reservations about it." I explained once more the reasons for which I believe I would be more useful if entrusted with an unofficial mission. Moreover, a change at the Vatican—as desirable as it may be—would be too late now. I wouldn't have time to build the required invaluable relationships and friendships. I know nobody there. It would be a completely different matter in Switzerland, where I have long-standing relationships. An unofficial mission there—for instance to the Red Cross—would enable me to obtain solid information. He agreed, but regretted that the insistence of a college friend had prevented him from offering me Berne, as he had meant to. The idea of a mission to the Red Cross, however, appealed to him, and he finally came round to it. As I was leaving he said, "I will talk tomorrow to Davidescu about your being representative to the Red Cross and Télémaque being appointed to the Vatican."

August 31. Davidescu called me in Sinaia, telling me to come without fail next day to Bucharest, to be received by Field Marshal Antonescu, because tomorrow morning the decree appointing me to the Vatican would be published. I told him that Mihai Antonescu and I had agreed that I would not be appointed to the Vatican, but would be entrusted with an unofficial mission. Davidescu replied, however, that the old project had been revived.

September 1. Davidescu confessed that it was he who had made Mihai Antonescu change his mind. He had explained to him that Rome would soon be occupied by the Allies, that Grigorcea would probably be obliged to follow the Italian government in its retreat, and that we could not leave as Romanian representative among the Anglo-Americans, of all people, Télémaque, known to be pro-German and a friend of von Papen. It was then definitively decided to send me to the Vatican. By arranging a meeting with the field marshal, one sought to force my hand!

Field Marshal Antonescu, with whom I spoke for half an hour, appeared sullen and depressed. After giving me some rather naïve instructions regarding my new mission, he began a defense of the policy he had followed. He had had to enter the war against Russia, since he could not stay with folded arms and receive Bessarabia as a gift from the Germans (or in exchange for Transylvania, which would have been even worse); he had had then to occupy Transdniestria and Crimea as security zones; he had similarly been forced to go up to the Donets and to Stalingrad, since when one is allied to a country one has to help it to the end. "You, the people who listen to the BBC, imagine perhaps that I am detested in London. But that is not so, because I did not make the same mistakes as Hitler; I did not persecute the Jews." He added: "Were I to listen to you all and withdraw our troops from the Kuban, what would the result be? Our troops' commanders would be shot by the Germans, as they shot the Italian generals who retreated in Sicily; the country would be occupied by the Germans and an Iron Guard government imposed, headed by Horia Sima or another Iron Guardist. Moreover, all of Transylvania would be handed over to the Hungarians. Let rather the Hungarians act foolishly so that we may take back our northern Transylvania. What I want is to recover during the war as many as possible of the lands that were snatched away from us, and then, at the peace conference, plead the cause of the integrity of Greater Romania's territory."

September 6. I went to say good-bye to Vişoianu. He was sorry that he could do nothing to save me from the onus of an official foreign mission while we have an Antonescu regime at the helm. He also regretted

Cretzianu going to Ankara. He will try to have me recommended to the American and British envoys wherever I will be, so that I may talk in the name of the opposition, that is, in the name of the people.

Last meeting with Cretzianu before our departures. We established a secret code between ourselves. We decided to remain at our posts as long as the king was on the throne. If Romania is occupied, we would declare that we represent the king, but that we refuse to have any contact with those in power in Bucharest, who keep our sovereign prisoner. If the king flees abroad, we would wait to see if he formed a government in exile, to which we would then adhere.

September 7. I paid a visit to Mihalache, who had expressed the wish to see me. Like the others, he believes that an unofficial mission for me would have been preferable. But since the only way I could plead abroad for Romania would be by heading our legation at the Vatican, both he and Maniu (in whose name he is authorized to speak to me) are of the opinion that I ought to accept the appointment. In Rome, I should speak not in the name of the present temporary government, but in that of the king and of the people, expressed by the two great opposition parties—National-Peasant and National-Liberal. The heads of these parties could let the British and American governments know that I speak in their names, so that my words would carry greater weight. It should be explained to the Anglo-Americans that an early withdrawal of Romanian troops from the Kuban (in any case, technically almost impossible to accomplish) or the overthrow of the Antonescu regime (easy to achieve) would immediately lead to the military occupation of Romania by the Germans, who would disarm our army, deport (or kill) the intellectual stratum, and lay hand on all our economic resources. The governments in London and Washington should carefully weigh the situation and give us their advice, which we would immediately follow, whatever it may be.

September 8. The Italian army capitulated without conditions.

Farewell visit to Mihai Antonescu. He greeted me with the words: "There is no longer any need to become Catholic; remain Orthodox, because there is no way now that you can reach Rome!" He added that I could carry out the same clarification and information activity in Switzerland. (I mentioned the Red Cross possibility, which appealed to him.) "It would be good for the British envoy in Switzerland to be informed that we have in Romania twenty-two partially armed divisions (their disposition is known to the Turks), forty carloads of gold, 400,000 carloads of wheat, 300,000 carloads of corn, petroleum, etc. A gesture by us (such as the withdrawal of our troops from the Kuban) would give all of these to the Germans, and probably lead to the liquidation of the pro-British circles. But when the Anglo-Americans reach our area, the change of governments will be made automatically, followed by an effective contribution to the Allied cause."

September 9. I paid a visit to Dinu Brătianu. He told me the same things as Mihalache. Be it at the Vatican or in Switzerland, I should try by all means to get in touch with the official representatives of Britain and the United States, in order to let them know of the real situation in Romania, of public sentiment, and of the opposition parties' decision. If, after considering all the consequences that would follow the overthrow of the Antonescu regime, the Allies were to recommend such an act, the opposition parties could, and would, do so: "We must do what the British tell us." He gave me a copy of a memorandum he had sent to Churchill; in case it hadn't been received, I could also forward a copy to London. In the afternoon, departure for Switzerland.

September 23. In Berne, I saw [Allen] Dulles (OSS representative at the American legation, former head of the State Department's Southeastern European Division). I described to him the king and the country's situation. I asked him whether it would be in the Allies' interest for Romania to change sides at this time. He took notes and will be in touch with Washington. He will try to invite me to lunch with Harrison (the American envoy) if the latter is allowed to attend. The British heads of mission are strictly forbidden to talk with diplomats of countries adhering to the Axis so as not to irritate the touchy Russians. Dulles is a very likable man, who laughs loudly and plays much golf. He said he would get in touch with me if he had something important to tell me.

September 27. I paid an official call on the International Committee of the Red Cross. I was received most warmly by Jacques Chenevière and Edouard Chapuisat, honorary citizen of Romania. They stated that among all national Red Cross societies, the Romanian was the one that collaborated most closely and rapidly with them. Chapuisat told me how well he had been received in Romania, and how he was able to visit many modern hospitals and first-rate health organizations. He considers the Dr. Cantacuzino Institute one of the best in the world. He was also allowed to visit the Jewish internment camps in Odessa, even though these in fact do not fall within the IRC's purview. He found that the Jews were not treated cruelly, but that their housing was not too salubrious because of overcrowding. He spoke about this with Field Marshal Antonescu, who immediately ordered that a few more villas be requisitioned, so that the internees have a bit more space. He told Mihai Antonescu how much harm this treatment of the Jews caused Romania; Mihai Antonescu blamed the field marshal and the Germans. These persecutions, unworthy of our times, should cease, Chapuisat told me. This was followed by a luncheon in my honor given by the IRC Committee at the Prado.

October 17. Because Gafencu phoned me that Dulles was coming to see him and that he insisted that I also be present, I went to Geneva. Dulles came and read to us the following cable he had received from Washington as answer to my communication:

1. The responsible circles of the United States have taken note of the information transmitted to the representative of the OSS by Mr. Raoul Bossy, Romanian minister designate to the Vatican.
2. Romania's position forms one of the subjects the United States Government is examining in consultation with its main Allies.
3. Although the only form of proposal the United States Government could take into serious consideration would be an offer of unconditional surrender made by an authorized representative of the Romanian government to the three principal Allies, there is, however, no reason preventing Mr. Dulles, representative of the OSS, from receiving, through the contact established in Switzerland, any subsequent approaches that the Romanians might wish to transmit by this means.
4. Meanwhile, the Allies cannot fail to pay attention to the fact that Romania continues to participate in the war against Russia and, more broadly, to any inimical action against the principal Allies, such as the treatment of the Jews, and of all the aspects of the collaboration with Germany.

I remarked that I found the tone rather harsh and somewhat unfair, since the communication I transmitted was on behalf of the king, of Maniu, and of Dinu Brătianu. To reproach them for the anti-Semitic measures and the collaboration with Germany does not seem right, since it is known that these persons have always fought against such tendencies. Dulles replied that the American government had also to express the official position, and that this was the first time that a direct and permanent contact with adversaries was accepted. As such, he said, the American reply had to be considered as extremely favorable. Later, I reminded Dulles that I had described the consequences of a Romanian change of policy in the present circumstances, and that I had asked we be told whether the overturn of the Antonescu regime at this time was deemed opportune. The fact that we received no reply means, in my view, that the Allied governments recognize that the king and opposition's caution is well founded and that they do not consider the moment appropriate for a policy change. Dulles, however, thought that the silence of the Allied governments on this point proved that they wanted to leave to us the responsibility of the initiative. I replied that I would understand that were only our interests concerned, but that I had asked whether it was in the *Allies'* interest. Since there had been no reply to this, it was clear the Allies do not consider it in their interest to have the overthrow take place now. Dulles had to agree that my interpretation was the right one, adding that the Allies could not define more precisely their attitude toward us before the Moscow conference.

November 22. Being told that Dulles had something urgent and important to tell me, I went to see him in Berne. He told me he had received from Washington a second answer to my message of September 23 (the first one, of October 17, being provisional ahead of the Moscow Conference). This answer was more or less as follows (he told it to me orally, he didn't read it): "After the discussions that took place at the Moscow Conference, the highest American authorities and the State Department in Washington consider that it would be useful, from their point of view, if Romania, through a properly accredited person, would sue for unconditional surrender. Such request should be addressed to the three principal Allied powers. This point of view has been adopted in Washington, even though it is realized that Romania is occupied by Germany. No assurances of any kind can be given to Romania."

Dulles added: "This is the answer given to Romania, and to Romania alone. It is presumable that, before stating it, the American government has been in touch with the British one, and also with Moscow. I realize the enormous responsibility that has to be taken in Bucharest. The king and Maniu might be taken as hostages, and so on. You have to think the matter over. In order not to carry alone the burden of the responsibility of transmitting such a communication, I would suggest, if I were you, that the American missions in Stockholm, Lisbon, and Ankara be approached in the same way, as their instructions are the same. I would also lay stress on the fact that no assurance whatever was given to you. Of course, Washington and London are speaking in their own interest. You have to study the matter in Bucharest and take your own risks, of course."

I told him the inevitable consequences: the rapid occupation by the Germans of all of Romania, the loss of all its riches, the abolition of the army. I drew his attention to the fact that for us the question was not to capitulate or not, but to overthrow the regime or not, because it was strongly believed in Romania that in the end Antonescu would not detach himself from Germany. "I know, I know," Dulles replied, "you have been very fair stating all that. All I can say is: the question has been studied at Moscow and afterward in Washington, and that is what I am authorized to give you as answer."

November 23. Gafencu phoned to say that Tilea, from London, sent a cable saying that President Beneš also advised us to take the expected step. But he asked that, before capitulating, we let him know. Gafencu infers from this that we are not viewed so badly and that we will be treated somewhat better than we had hoped.

December 31. During dinner, G. Anastasiu, from the legation in Berne, phoned to tell me he has received a letter from Niculescu-Buzeşti, who asked him to let me know that all my confidential reports had been forwarded to "the responsible level" (the king, Maniu, Dinu Brătianu), who warmly congratulate me for them and wish that I continue filing them.

1944

January 1. I read Field Marshal Antonescu's message to the country. He no longer speaks of victory, of anti-Bolshevik crusade, of Pan-Slavic peril. If only he had not mentioned them earlier! He tries to justify his policy. He sent troops across the Dniester "because you cannot abandon your ally as soon as you have reached your personal goals." It all depends on who your ally is! If that ally mercilessly dismembered your country, if in the thick of war he made not a single move to lighten the yoke of your brothers he drove into slavery, I think you too have the right to follow the policy that best serves your interests.

January 12. Ciano was shot yesterday in Verona, along with old Field Marshal de Bono. One fact is certain: Mussolini's political career is over.

February 24. Kopecki (permanent delegate of Czechoslovakia to the League of Nations and representative of President Beneš in Switzerland) showed me two cables he had received from London that contain Tilea's message for Maniu (via Gafencu). He learned that Stalin had expressed relatively favorable sentiments toward Romania in his discussions with Beneš in Moscow. Stalin told Beneš that what he was asking from Romania was the 1940 borders without any enlargement, that is, without the Danube's mouth or Dobrudja as had been rumored. In exchange, he undertakes to ensure that all of Transylvania is returned to Romania. As Romanian government, Stalin would want a Maniu government. He would like Transylvanians (not the "boyars" from Bucharest) to have the major voice in the leadership of the Romanian government, because they are more sincerely attached to democratic principles than those from the Old Kingdom. The above conditions, however, refer only to an unconditional surrender, and are valid only were we to detach ourselves from the Germans before the Russian army crosses the Dniester. I replied that the loss of Bessarabia and of northern Bukovina, with its major intellectual center of Cernăuţi, is a great sacrifice we are asked for, and to which I did not know whether the Romanian people would ever consent. Kopecki understood our grief, but asked us to realize that in its present tragic situation, Romania's sole preoccupation must be "to save what it can save," rather than to stick to an intransigent position that could lead to "the loss of everything."

March 20. Yesterday, Soviet troops crossed the Dniester and, today, they occupied Soroca.

March 21. The German army occupied Hungary today.

March 22. Under German pressure, Horthy dismissed Kallay and appointed General Döme Sztójay, my former colleague in Berlin, as prime minister and foreign minister.

June 5. The Allies have occupied Rome today.

June 6. The beginning of the Allies' invasion in Europe. Troops under the command of the American general Eisenhower debarked this morning at 6:00 A.M. on the northern coast of France, in Normandy.

June 12. The Allied bridgehead in Normandy seems definitely and solidly established. The bombing of Ploeşti continues.

July 14–15. Pella [Romanian envoy to Switzerland] phoned me that I have been appointed to the Coordination Committee of the Ministry of Foreign Affairs, assigned to coordinate our legations in Berlin, Stockholm, Helsingfors, and Prague. I wrote to him asking that my appointment be rescinded, since I was unable to leave Switzerland.

July 21. Pella called to tell me I was being urgently summoned to Bucharest to take part in the work of the Coordination Committee. If I demurred, I should clarify my position, since for the past six months I was considered to be on leave. I replied that if the mission of representative to the International Committee of the Red Cross in Geneva was not seen as sufficient to justify my absence from the country, I would prefer to be placed on leave without pay. Pella insisted that I give the matter more thought and that I let him fix up things; he added that he would offer me a solution in a couple of days.

July 22. Failed attempt on Hitler's life and bloody reprisals. Something, it seems, has begun to move in Germany. The army's opposition to the Nazis is stiffening.

July 25. Pella phoned me the text of the cable he intended to send Mihai Antonescu. He proposed that I either remain as representative to the Red Cross or that I be appointed to the Coordination Committee but with a leave of six months. I answered that I would go along with his text, provided he deleted the Coordination Committee solution and the request for a six-month leave. I also sent him a letter in which I stated that, being unable to leave Switzerland at this time, I was asking either that my mission at the Red Cross be recognized as an assignment by the Ministry or that I be placed on leave without pay. *Alea jacta est!*

August 2. Turkey has broken diplomatic relations with Germany. The dawn of our exit from the war approaches!

August 3. In Finland, President Ryti was forced to resign and was replaced by Mannerheim, who has already arranged that peace negotiations with Russia be resumed.

August 15. The third Allied invasion of Europe has begun, on the southern coast of France.

Pella called to tell me that my request for a leave of absence without pay had been turned down, and that I was included in the Ministry's new staff listing, but without any indication of assignment.

August 17. The Allies are twenty-three kilometers from Paris. Momentous days! As I was saying in 1939: immanent justice will prevail.

August 22. Jassy has been occupied by the Russians.

August 23. Paris was liberated today.

In a proclamation, King Michael announced that Romania has accepted Russia's peace proposals, that a new Romanian government was formed under the leadership of Maniu and Dinu Brătianu (apparently under the nominal presidency of General Sănătescu), and that Romania now goes to war against Germany, alongside its allies of 1914–1918.

August 24. The news from Romania becomes more specific. A government of national unity has been formed by the Liberal, National-Peasant, Socialist, and Communist parties. General Sănătescu, head of the king's military house, is prime minister and has as ministers of state Maniu, Dinu Brătianu, Titel Petrescu (Socialist), and Pătraşcanu (Communist). The king announced that the Allies recognize Romania's independence and the unfairness of the Vienna arbitral award, and that, with the help of the Allied army, Romania will reconquer Transylvania.

The American Dulles and the Czechoslovak Kopecki phone to congratulate me most warmly for the step taken by my country.

August 25. The Romanian military command told the German military command in Romania that, in consequence of our decision to end the war against the United Nations, it should withdraw as quickly as possible from the country, and it guaranteed that it could do so in safety. The German military command accepted these conditions but, breaking its word, it massed troops at Băneasa, with a view to disarming the Romanian units in Bucharest, bombed the city, and machine-gunned the civilian population. The Romanian government consequently told the German legation that, by these violent acts, the Reich had put itself in a state of war with Romania. Romania from now on finds itself in the ranks of the Allies—as it should have from the beginning. I cabled the king, through Alexander Cretzianu in Ankara, expressing my unshakable loyalty to him.

August 27. Gallin, my former consul general in Berlin, the last Romanian to have arrived from Germany, came to see me. He told me that the attempt against Hitler's life has produced intense satisfaction in the Reich, for it showed at last some reaction to the "madman's" tyranny. The hanging of the generals has shocked public opinion. Only some fanatic SS still believe in the possibility of victory. An internal revolution seems, however, out of the question because of the Gestapo. What one will see instead is a disintegration of the army, which, no longer willing to fight, will gradually surrender on the different fronts, as can already be seen in France, Romania, Russia, and Italy.

September 5. King Michael has re-established the democratic constitution of 1923, the conception of which I witnessed as political director of the Council of the Presidency under Ion I.C. Brătianu. That constitution, so strongly opposed by Maniu at that time, is now being brought back into force by the selfsame Maniu!

Brussels has been liberated. Allied troops have crossed the German and Dutch borders.

September 7. Romania declares war on Hungary, in order to recover northern Transylvania. Russia declares war on Bulgaria (perhaps in order also to take part in the armistice negotiations with the Allies).

September 13. The armistice with the Allies was signed yesterday in Moscow. Romania cedes Bessarabia and northern Bukovina, but in exchange it receives the guarantee of recovering all (or most of) Transylvania.

September 21. I receive a thank-you cable from the king, in response to the cable I sent him when he overthrew the nefarious Antonescu regime.

October 7. I had lunch with Bielle Stîrcea, who described the coup in Romania. A conversation accidentally overheard by Ion Stîrcea at his physician's revealed the necessity of bringing forward the date of the coup (initially set for August 26), because Field Marshal Antonescu was planning to leave for Moldavia on the 24th. August 23 was chosen, when Antonescu was called to the Palace. He was received by the king in the presence of General Sănătescu, while Ionel Stîrcea, Buzeşti, and Ioaniţiu (the king's young schoolmate) stood watch behind the door, revolvers in hand, ready to intervene in case of danger. The king told Antonescu that he had forthwith to conclude an armistice with Russia. Antonescu replied that he had first to obtain an Anglo-American guarantee against the USSR. The king pointed out that one could not ask London and Washington for a guarantee against one of their allies, and therefore that he had to ask for an armistice or tender his resignation. Antonescu refused both solutions in a rude tone. And as he became more and more intemperate, despite Sănătescu's efforts to calm him down, the king left the room and told Stîrcea, Buzeşti, and Ioaniţiu to warn the royal guard that, at the given signal, it was to arrest the "Conducător." The king returned to his office. Antonescu was shouting that things would not happen that easily, and so forth. The king then pressed a bell under his desk, and his three above-mentioned collaborators entered with the royal guard. Seeing that he was being arrested, Antonescu spat on the officer in charge and yelled, "Tomorrow morning you will all be shot." But he was pushed toward the staircase by the soldiers and imprisoned in one of the Palace's anti-aircraft shelters.

Learning what had happened, Killinger came and was immediately received by the king. It was a painful meeting: the German, insolent, hands on hips, threatening the king with the grave consequences that awaited him. Then Hansen and Gerstenberg came to see Sănătescu, promising a peaceful withdrawal of the German army, and asking for themselves a laissez-passer. With the help of this document, they went to the Băneasa airport, from which they had the Luftwaffe bomb Bucharest, and especially the Royal Palace.

October 23. All of Transylvania has been reconquered.

December 7. The new Romanian government headed by General Nicolae Rădescu has essentially the same composition as the outgoing one headed by General Sănătescu.

1945

January 1. The legation in Berne received a cable from the Foreign Ministry announcing my appointment as honorary representative of the Romanian government to the International Committee of the Red Cross (until now, I was only representative of the Romanian Red Cross Society).

February 14. Budapest is taken by Russo-Romanian troops. In Romania, there have been large Communist demonstrations. They were opposed by an even larger demonstration in favor of the government, at which Rădescu gave a speech full of good sense.

February 28. Following a series of bloody demonstrations directed by Ana Pauker, and of some radio allocutions by General Rădescu—energetic, brave, full of common sense if not of political sense—Rădescu was forced to resign. Vyshinsky, deputy commissar for foreign affairs of the USSR, arrives in Bucharest to oversee the constitution of the new government, for, as we are reminded by London, we are not yet accepted in the ranks of co-belligerents and therefore the constitution of a government requires, in addition to the royal consent, also that of the Allies.

March 7. The new Romanian government is headed by Petru Groza, with Tătărescu as his deputy and foreign minister. It is a government composed solely of members of the National Democratic Front and of four Dissident Liberals. The traditional Liberals and the National-Peasants refuse to join this government.

April 29. Mussolini and seventeen of his collaborators were shot near Como and their bodies displayed in a square in Milan.

May 1. The German radio announces Hitler's death. Disease? Assassination? Suicide? Or deception to conceal a flight? It is, however, likely that he is dead. Thus vanishes from the face of the earth the most sinister criminal, in whose wake the world remains ruined, exhausted, irremediably stricken in the flower of its youth. Six years of catastrophes and all of Romania's calamities are all due to him and to the evil forces he unleashed.

May 2. The fall of Berlin. The greatest defeat in German history, and a rightful revenge for Paris, Prague, Vienna, Warsaw, Brussels, The

Hague, Oslo, Copenhagen, Belgrade, and Athens. The German army in Italy and the Tyrol has capitulated. Field Marshal Rundstedt and former ambassador von Mackensen have surrendered to the Allied troops. I clearly recall when Mackensen, in Venice, in the spring of 1940, rose beamingly during a luncheon at the Danieli to announce to everyone that "the German flag floats over Liège." What a great feat for a state armed to the teeth to vanquish a small, but brave, country!

May 8. V-E Day. This morning, an impressive service and Te Deum at the Anglican church in Territet.

August 10. Japan has capitulated unconditionally.

August 23. First anniversary of Romania's change of sides in favor of the United Nations. Reception at our legation in Berne. People are quite excited and optimistic because of the brave, and very skillful, action in response to the recent speech of the British foreign minister, Bevin, who stated that the Romanian, Bulgarian, and Hungarian governments would not be recognized and admitted into the United Nations unless they were constituted on genuinely democratic bases. The king then asked the representatives of Britain, the U.S., and the USSR to help him constitute a government that would fulfill the conditions necessary to be recognized by the Allies. The king's decision was taken only after it had proved impossible to dismiss the Groza government. Washington and London, basing themselves on the Yalta agreement, declared to be ready to begin the negotiations requested by King Michael. From Moscow, however, one hears only praise of the Groza government, denoting an attitude hostile to the views of the Romanian monarch.

September 10. *Izvestia* accuses Britain and the United States of having pressured King Michael to appeal to the three great powers against the Groza government. In reply, United Press discloses how this government was violently imposed on the king by Vyshinsky.

October 8–9. The government has recalled Cretzianu from Ankara, but he refuses to comply, since there was no decree recalling him (because King Michael has stopped signing decrees since he no longer recognizes the Groza government, which refuses to step down).

October 28. Lunch at Gafencu's, with Caranfil, Antoniade, and Assan. The Groza government has recalled from abroad and dismissed forty-seven diplomats and members of related services, foremost among them Gafencu and Cretzianu. I propose that we, those who have not yet been subjected to such a measure, cable Bucharest to show solidarity with those stricken, to reject a discrimination in our favor, and to state that we intend to share our colleagues' fate. Gafencu is categorically opposed to my view, which is shared only by Liviu Cicio-Pop, the only secretary of the Berne legation not to have been dismissed. Gafencu says that the affected diplomats do not recognize the legitimacy of the government's measure, since no decree of recall has been signed by the king, while the Groza government itself, having been dismissed by the king, has no constitutional legitimacy. Cretzianu, in Ankara, and Brutus Coste, in Lisbon, consider themselves to be still in office and will not vacate the buildings of their respective legations. Were we to resign, therefore, we would seem to recognize the legality of the dismissals.

October 30. Gafencu continues to be vigorously opposed to my suggestion of showing solidarity with my dismissed colleagues. The Americans from the legation in Berne—and Joyce in particular—told him that we must all stay in our positions so as not to make room for the Communists.

December 20. At their conference in Moscow, "the Big Three" decided to advise King Michael, in reply to his letter of August 23, "to enlarge his present government by the inclusion of one representative from each of the National-Peasant and Liberal parties." Vyshinsky (deputy commissar for foreign affairs of the USSR), Clark Kerr (ambassador of Britain), and Harriman (ambassador of the U.S.) have gone to Bucharest to help the king effect this reshuffling. It is a second "Munich."

1946

January 1. In Romania, the crisis continues. The government does not accept to include Dinu Brătianu and Mihalache as representatives of the historic parties.

January 8. Emil Haţieganu and M. Romniceanu have entered the government, the first as representative of the National-Peasant party, the second of the Liberals. But Maniu, in an interview, thundered and fulminated against this formula, which does not change the government's nature and forces the king to collaborate with a rebel government submissive to a foreign country. The détente thus appears precarious and has no other purpose than to allow the king to end his "strike."

January 10. A cable from the Foreign Ministry, signed by Tătărescu, puts an end to my *governmental* mission to the Red Cross as of January 15,[1]

[1]But Bossy continues to represent the Romanian Red Cross Society until late 1947.

and tells me to "return urgently to Romania for a new assignment." The times of tribulation start again. Taking back my family being an impossibility, either I remain here with them, or I leave with the prospect of a very long separation. Grigore Gafencu and Dinu Hiott advise me to stay, "temporize without burning your bridges." I therefore request a medical leave.

January 25. I received from Eddie Boxshall, from London, the following cable: "Just returned from Bucharest. Robert[2] wishes you to know that the job the Ministry will offer you is secretary-general, when the present holder [of the office] leaves for Washington. Meantime, probably Head of the Political Department. Your friends state it is impossible [for them] to advise you, for or against. They consider you must decide yourself whether to return."

February 5. The British and American governments told the Groza government that they wanted to recognize it.

March 3. A phone call from the legation in Berne informs me that the following cable was received for me: "Foreign Minister Tătărescu has refused the leave requested through Mr. Franasovici."[3]

March 6. Great speech by Churchill in Fulton (Missouri) in which he emphasizes the Communist and Russian dangers.

March 7. New cable from Stoica, received through the legation in Berne, in which he informs me that Tătărescu is repeating his recall order. This time, I do not answer.

March 9. I receive a touching letter from N. Caranfil, in which he encourages and congratulates me for not submitting to the injunctions of the present government in Bucharest. "One cannot make too great a sacrifice for freedom, and especially for that of one's country." He also has words of praise for Senta, "your wonderful companion." I must recognize that her courage, her smiling dignity in the face of the difficulties and dangers of our life are indeed admirable; such a statement might seem lacking in modesty on the part of a husband, but if my children later read these pages, I want them to know what a brave and generous mother they have.

May 18. The people's tribunal in Bucharest condemned to death the Antonescus and some of their close collaborators. They may have erred, but traitors they were not.

---

[2]General Robert Bossy, the author's brother.

[3]Franasovici had received the demand on January 15, as he was leaving for Romania, but failed to deliver it until early March.

September 17–21. At the Peace Conference in Paris the issue of Transylvania is resolved to our full satisfaction. In other matters, and especially in that of reparations, we are pitilessly sacrificed to the greed of the more powerful.

December 1. The Romanian elections apparently gave Maniu 85 percent of the votes. But the government announced that it had won 71 percent. What a tragicomedy.

December 28. A few days ago, on December 19, our Legation in Berne sent me yet another cable from Tătărescu, asking me to return immediately to Romania "in order to be given a new assignment." As last year, I replied, also through the legation, explaining that while desirous to return to Romania, for family reasons I could not do so now.

Not long afterward, the author was dismissed from the Romanian diplomatic corps and, later still, deprived of his citizenship by the Communists.

14

Exile (1947–1975)

Thus ended the official diplomatic career of Raoul Bossy. He remained active, however, during most of his twenty-eight years of exile in Switzerland, Canada, the United States, France, and again Switzerland, where he died of cancer at the age of eighty. He was buried in the cemetery of Saanen, surrounded by the mountains of his beloved Switzerland.

He continued, among his various activities, to do his best to ease the sufferance of the Romanians caught in the whirlwind of those times. As representative of the Romanian Red Cross to the International Committee of the Red Cross, at first he looked as best he could after the well-being of Romanian prisoners of war in the Soviet Union and in Germany. He arranged for food and warm clothing to be sent to them—and also to Romanian diplomats interned in Germany—often from stocks of the British and American Red Cross societies.

After the end of the war, his efforts turned to having aid shipments sent to Romania—especially for the starving children of Moldavia—and to helping the growing wave of refugees reaching Western Europe. He participated in various Red Cross conferences as representative of the Romanian Society, including one in Oxford in 1946 where, at the suggestion of Basil O'Connor, president of the American Red Cross Society and president of the Council of Governors of the League of Red Cross Societies, he was unanimously elected president of the Commission for the Revision of the Statutes. At about this time, too, he began a vigorous campaign, through the Red Cross and—especially—through the World

Council of Churches, to reduce the terrible mistreatment of political prisoners in Aiud and in the growing number of other Romanian concentration camps.

In the meantime, assisted by the Soviet army, the Romanian Communists were gradually taking over the entire country. In July 1947 Maniu and Mihalache were arrested for "treason" and later sentenced to life imprisonment; the National-Peasant party was outlawed. In September, failing after several months to browbeat the Romanian Red Cross into submission, the Communist government abolished by fiat the Central and Executive Committees of the Red Cross and replaced them by a "Provisional Commission" consisting of members of governmental parties, with no grounding in the subject matter; this commission almost immediately began sending to the Greek Communist guerrillas the gifts received from the American Red Cross to relieve misery in Romania. And in late December 1947, the Communists forced King Michael to abdicate and leave the country.

Even though this Provisional Commission would have liked him to remain as its representative to the International Red Cross, Bossy considered it totally out of the question to act for a Communist commission that, moreover, was depriving the Romanian population by diverting aid stocks to the Greek rebels. Instead, with a group of other Romanians connected with the legal Red Cross, he founded the Committee for the Assistance of Romanian Refugees (Caroman), and he established close relations with the League of Red Cross Societies, the International Refugee Office (IRO), the Ecumenical Council, and other nongovernmental organizations represented in Geneva.

He worked especially closely with the IRO and the Ecumenical Council, in particular for the resettlement of intellectual refugees from Eastern Europe. He represented the Ecumenical Council and the Commission of Churches for International Affairs in the drafting of the "Migrant's Charter" for the Union of Nongovernmental Organizations. He fought hard to improve the miserable lot of Romanian escapees in Yugoslavia and to secure their immigration to Western Europe. In June 1948 he was elected vice president of the Caroman, in March 1950 its president. A year later, because he was on the point of emigrating to Canada, he passed the presidency on to Marie Brăescu.

Bossy was also very active in the European movement through his membership in the Romanian National Federalist Council and the European Union of Federalists. By contrast, he did not get involved in the political squabbles among Romanian refugees. These resulted from the puffed-up egos and hopeless ambitions of politicians who were separated not by ideology (except for the Iron Guard's remnants, who were shunned by all), but by personal feuds. Bossy was dismayed by the selfishness and lack of patriotism of men who should have set aside petty jealousies to fight united for the freedom of their country, and he was also distressed by the fact that he had close childhood friends in each of the two camps. His neutrality was at first seen badly by the two camps, each of which obviously considered him to be siding with the opposite group. But little by little they realized that he was merely remaining neutral, that he was not seeking any personal gain, and that he was always ready to be of assistance. One result of this neutrality was that he was sought out several times by American officials who wished to get an impartial and objective assessment of the Romanian refugee world.

As time passed, it became clear that exile would last for a long time, and Bossy began to focus on the future of his family. Most of his children were now reaching working age, and foreigners could not obtain work permits in Europe at that time. Emigrating overseas thus became a necessity. When the National Committee for a Free Europe asked him in late 1950 whether he was willing to join the center it was setting up in Munich, he turned the offer down for the sake of his children's future. But when the Refugee Department of the Ecumenical Council offered him a short-term assignment to organize in Toronto, with the help of the Canadian Council of Churches, the immigration of Eastern Orthodox intellectual refugees from Eastern Europe, he accepted in the hope that his children would be able to build their lives in North America.

In May 1951, brokenhearted, he left Europe for Canada with part of his family and settled in Toronto. When his short-term position with the Ecumenical Council came to an end, he undertook an intensive schedule of speeches and broadcasts throughout eastern Canada, organized mainly by the Canadian Institute of International Affairs, and also published a number of articles. He participated in an unofficial capacity in the International Red Cross's meeting in Toronto, where he was warmly greeted by numerous acquaintances (as he had been when he visited Ottawa), and he represented Paris's Carol I Foundation at the celebration of Laval University's centenary. During trips to the United States he established contacts with various organizations there, and recorded several speeches at Radio Free Europe for transmission to Romania.

In December 1952, Bossy was appointed to the editorial board of the *Cronica Românească,* the Romanian political journal issued by the National Committee for a Free Europe, and he immediately left Toronto to assume his new position in New York, where he was later joined by most of his family. In 1954 Free Europe transferred him from Free Europe Press to its academic branch, the Mid-European Studies Center. Later that year, he also began collaborating with the Voice of America, sending it weekly scripts of comments on international political developments, for transmission to Romania.

At the suggestion of the Free Europe Committee, exiles from behind the Iron Curtain began working in August 1954 on the creation of an Assembly of Captive European Nations (ACEN) through a group of coordinators, one for each country. The Free Europe Committee suggested Bossy as coordinator for the Romanians, and both Romanian feuding factions seconded this nomination. The coordinators worked steadily for a month, drawing up the statutes. They decided that each national group would have sixteen members, and also included four international political organizations—the Agrarians, the Christian Democrats, the Liberals, and the Socialists—with four members each. The Romanian delegation was composed of members of the two feuding groups. The thorniest issue was that of the inclusion of the Yugoslavs, which was strenuously opposed by the United States because of its "flirt" with Tito; the outcome was that the Yugoslavs were included "in principle," but that the means of their inclusion would be examined at a later date. The first session of the ACEN was held on September 20–22, 1954, at the Carnegie Endowment International Center, across the street from the United Nations, which had just started its own session. Bossy was elected to the ACEN's Political Commission, and later to that Commission's vice presidency.

Bossy continued to hold himself aloof from the infighting among the two groups of Romanian refugees, each of which wanted to co-opt him. When, in early 1955, a Romanian National Committee was finally established, its head, Vişoianu, came to ask him to join it, his name being on a list approved by the king. Bossy thanked him, but said he was unable to accept the offer because the committee's proposed membership reflected too much a single political party, the National-Peasant one. (Besides, he tended to look down upon the tussle among his compatriots for membership in the Committee, which he characterized as a "vanity fair.") But he added that he was prepared to continue working within the Romanian delegation to the ACEN—which he did for the next decade, until he left for Europe.

Gradually, however, Bossy became disillusioned with the line pursued by the ACEN. The acceptance of the satellite countries into the United Nations and its specialized organizations and, more generally, the attitudes of Western governments and public opinions, led Bossy to question the efficacy of following a hard, intransigent line. He did his share in lobbying delegates to the United Nations, in making speeches and writing letters to the editor, but he was a proponent of a more flexible and realistic approach. He appeared to agree with Ambassador François-Poncet's characterization of the ACEN leaders, which Bossy recorded in his diary, as being "mediocre, aged, rusty, incapable of understanding the present situation, seemingly living in the past." And in the spring of 1964, at a symposium organized by the Free Europe Committee at Princeton University, Bossy showed, as mentioned in his diary: "the stupidity of the attitude adopted by the ACEN . . . which fancies it can change the American government's policy and that of the other Western powers seeking to detach the satellite regimes from Moscow's clutches through economic and cultural ties. I proposed, on the contrary, that we take reality into account and that we collaborate with the Western governments, suggesting the benefits they should seek in exchange for the tightening of those economic and cultural ties that would hasten the process of "detaching from Moscow" the captive nations. . . . The Americans, Poles, and Hungarians agreed with me; the others remained silent."

While Free Europe, the Voice of America, and the ACEN kept Bossy busy, he nevertheless found time to take full advantage of what New York had to offer. He was in particular happy to meet again and collaborate with old friends and acquaintances from behind the Iron Curtain, such as Tibor Eckhardt, George Bakách-Bessenyey, Leon Orlowski, and so many others. He was also happy to meet once more the many foreign diplomats he had befriended in earlier years and who, often after several promotions, were now either posted to the United Nations or passing through New York. He felt especially close to the French community in New York, being frequently invited to the French embassy and being elected a member of the Council of the Alliance Française.

In 1956, he was invited to lecture in Paris at the Carol I Foundation and at the International Free Academy of Science and Letters, of both of which he was a member. The Free Europe Committee considered both cycles of lectures to be very useful and assisted in the financing of the trip, which extended over a period of almost two months. Bossy took advantage of his stay in Paris to meet again with many of his former colleagues, mainly French—such as François-Poncet—but also of other nationalities, as well as with marking personalities among the Romanian refugees in France.

The same trip was repeated in 1958, with a new schedule of lectures for the International Free Academy of Science and Letters and the Carol I Foundation, as well as with renewed meetings with former foreign colleagues and Romanian refugees. Thereafter, these trips became annual affairs, and Bossy added to them vacations in several European countries. He also contributed over the years a number of articles to learned French journals.

In September 1965, Radio Free Europe offered Bossy the position of political commentator at its Paris studio, an offer he hastened to accept. Though he was not unhappy in the United States, he did yearn for Europe and for whatever whiff of pre–World War I atmosphere it could provide. He took up residence alone in his beloved St. Germain-des-Prés district, for his family had by now settled down in jobs or academic endeavors, and he continued to associate with his old friends while writing his weekly political commentaries.

The last entry in his diaries is dated July 9, 1969. It was around that time he was diagnosed with an incurable cancer. He was joined by his wife, who gave up her teaching career in New York, and they settled down in Switzerland, where he died on August 31, 1975.

Thus ended a long life whose brilliant career was cut short in midcourse, to be followed by many years of vicissitudes and financial straits. Bossy's remaining hope in those years of dejection was to see his children take root and forge new and successful lives for themselves. In that he fully succeeded.

Appendix A
The Life of Ferdinand I

The ruler who, on the day of his enthronement, had pledged to be "a good Romanian and king" did not owe his throne to a fortuitous and automatic dynastic succession. He had *willed* himself sovereign of the Romanians, to whom he had felt bound from the first encounter when, still a boy, he had accompanied his father and older brother to Romania to attend the coronation of his uncle, Carol I. Later, the old king, having no descendants, decided to choose a successor from within his own family. His mind had been set on the youngest of his brother Leopold's three sons, the one who was his godchild and his namesake. He therefore asked Leopold, the head of the Hohenzollern House, to persuade his two eldest sons, Wilhelm and Ferdinand, to renounce their eventual rights to the Romanian crown so that his godson might inherit it. Wilhelm readily agreed to his uncle's proposal, but the second son, Ferdinand, objected, saying that destiny intended him to continue the Romanian dynasty founded by Carol I, and he did not want to turn away from this lofty responsibility. And it is thus that, when the time came, Ferdinand became king of Romania, not only by the grace of God and the will of the nation, but also by his own free will.

His reign was short, but dramatic and glorious. A gentle soul, unassuming and reserved, full of an aristocratic distinction and of that shyness found so often in royal offspring, his conscience was abruptly confronted, from his first day on the throne, by the most perturbing and tormenting question. The Hohenzollerns were brought up, from father to son, in devotion to duty, honor, and loyalty. In that hour of terrible doubt, of tragic moral struggle, Ferdinand I felt in the innermost depth of his conscience that his duty was to disregard his ties to the past—to his family, to his native country, to the army in which he had served as a youth—and to put himself entirely at the service of the nation that, although it knew he was of foreign extraction, had placed its trust in him. With his conscience torn between two duties of fidelity, he erased from his heart the tender memories of Sigmaringen, the image of the medieval castle on a hilltop and of the surrounding forests full of fairy tales and legends, he relegated to oblivion the old glittering uniform of a Prussian officer—so dear to the Hohenzollerns—and he unsheathed the sword to reunify the nation. Handsome are the words then uttered by the new king: "Since I was able to defeat the Hohenzollern in me, I shall know how to vanquish the enemy." Although born and brought up in foreign parts and so strikingly different from the people over whom he ruled by his mentality and behavior, his Nordic features, his German accent, even his elongated Nordic handwriting, Ferdinand Hohenzollern nevertheless merged his soul with that of the Romanians and made for them the greatest of sacrifices in order to help fulfill their national aspiration.

And it was thus that the German princeling born at the sources of the Danube became not only a good but a great Romanian and king, who sealed with his name the high point of the Romanian epic by being crowned in Alba Iulia the first king of all the Romanians. In domestic policy he followed in the footsteps of one of his great predecessors to the throne, Prince Alexandru Ion Cuza, by ensuring that the peasants owned the land they tilled. And in order to set the example from above, he insisted that the Crown lands not be exempted from expropriation.

The crown of laurels that adorned the brow of him whom the people called "the King of Reunification," or "the King of the Peasants," was, however, intertwined with a crown of thorns. In his private life, Ferdinand I tasted in full from the cup of bitterness. Uprooted from the region he was born and raised in, transplanted in surroundings so different from those in which he had lived, deprived in an austere and rigid court of the carefree joys of youth, prevented from marrying his Romanian fiancée, Elena Văcărescu, by the famed "this ain't possible" of Lascar Catargi, Ferdinand's life seemed managed, over his hesitant and timid protestations, by his canny and cold uncle. The arrival in our parts, from distant British shores, of the fair-haired princess who was to be his wife, was for the heir apparent, as well as for all Romanians, like a sunbeam portending a great future for the country and a dynasty closely bound to the Romanian people. The young princess was immediately infused with faith in the destiny of the nation to which she was going to devote her life and which she was going to depict to the world with her brilliant gift as a writer. This unshakable faith gave her the strength to hearten her royal spouse when, called to the throne at one of history's major turning points, he had to disregard his feelings in order to live up to his duty.

King Ferdinand also had to experience, in the first phase of the war of emancipation, the agonies of retreat and of a humiliating peace that would have undermined the country's future and to which, for that reason, he did not officially give his royal assent. And in those days of heavy trials, the beautiful and brave Queen Marie strenuously guarded against the doubts and despair that might have insinuated themselves in people's hearts. She was the beacon that, even in the darkest of nights, never went out.

The hour of redemption finally struck, however, with the victory of our arms, the reestablishment of the nation within its rightful borders, and the glory of the coronation in Alba Iulia. But later, hurt in his family life and saddened by the events that shook the dynasty, the old king succumbed at the height of his prestige as sovereign to a pitiless and unforgiving disease, at a time when his hand was needed more than ever at the helm of the state. I was certain that the glorious image of Ferdinand I, surrounded by the halo of his human suffering, would forever remain dear to the nation over which he reigned for thirteen years.

Appendix B
Bárdossy's Draft of a Secret Romano-Hungarian Protocol

CONFIDENTIAL DRAFT

CONFIDENTIAL PROTOCOL

H.E. Mr. Victor Antonescu, minister of foreign affairs of Romania, on the one part, and Mr. László Bárdossy, envoy extraordinary and minister plenipotentiary of Hungary, on the other part, prompted by the wish to see a consolidation of existing relations between their two countries and thereby to make an effective contribution to the upholding of peace in Europe generally, and in Central Europe in particular,

having undertaken talks on this matter,

have agreed on the procedure to be followed in order to achieve the objective here-above recalled [*sic*] by undersigning in this Confidential Protocol the agreement thus reached.

I

The Royal Government of Romania, along with the governments of its allies, Czechoslovakia and Yugoslavia, will declare on its own initiative and without any conditions that it considers null and void the military, naval, and aerial clauses of the Treaty of Trianon, and that it recognizes Hungary's full equality of rights in armament matters. This declaration, the text of which is annexed to the present Protocol, shall be published on September __, 1937.

II

The Government of Hungary will declare that it renounces any use of force in its relations with the neighboring States.

This Declaration will be followed by a similar declaration, toward Hungary, by the Royal Government of Romania, as well as by the governments of its allies, Czechoslovakia and Yugoslavia.

This Declaration, the texts of which are annexed to the present Protocol, shall be published consecutively within two days of the Declaration alluded to in article I.

III

The Royal Government of Romania will get in touch as soon as possible with the authorized representatives of the Hungarian minority, and especially with those of the Magyar party in Romania, to agree with them and resolve all the remaining disputes, so as to secure for the Romanian citizens belonging to the Hungarian minority the treatment, as well as all the freedoms and rights, that are their due according to the principles of equality and equity and, likewise, to ensure the free practice of their religions, the free use of their language, of their customs, and of their institutions, that were guaranteed by the provisions of the treaty signed between Romania and the Principal Allied and Associated Powers on December 9, 1919.

Signed in _____ on _____, 1937

CONFIDENTIAL NOTE

I

Cancellation of the measures (administrative changes in the agricultural property records) infringing on the property rights concerning certain real estates of the so-called *Status Romanus Catholicus Transylvaniensis* of the Catholic Diocese of Roman rite of Alba Iulia, of the religious orders of the Premonstratensians, of the Piarists, and of the Minor Brothers, as well as of the Reformed Church; restoration of the previous situation for these assets, in fact and in law, including restoration in the agricultural property records; discontinuance of judicial and extra-judicial procedures that have been instituted against the assets in question.

II

Lifting of attachment of certain collections and certain assets belonging to the Association of the Museum of Transylvania (E.M.E.). Settlement of this Association's situation and assets.

III

Measures required to ensure that the schools, religious associations, or charities established and maintained by the Hungarian minority, receive an equitable share of the sums that are being or will be disbursed for that purpose from the budgets of the state, of the municipalities, or of others.

IV

In the localities where a considerable proportion of the inhabitants are Romanian citizens belonging to the Hungarian minority and where this minority maintains a confessional school—exemption of the taxpayers of that minority from any taxation (taxes to cover the costs of building and maintaining a public school).

V

Prohibition of all methods (analyses of surnames, compulsory enrollments, etc.) liable to prevent Romanian citizens belonging to the Hungarian minority from enrolling their children in schools other than those chosen by themselves [*sic*].

VI

Ending of the campaign to Romanianize citizens belonging to the Hungarian minority, particularly in the so-called "Szekler" districts.

VII

Ending of the proselytism aimed at converting Romanian citizens belonging to religious minorities (Roman Catholic, Reformed, Unitarian, etc.).

VIII

Review of the authorizations to publish scholastic textbooks. Prohibition of the use (rescinding of authorizations) of books that, concerning the Hungarian people and nation, contain statements liable to disturb the harmony between citizens belonging to the majority and those belonging to the minority, and to foster a sentiment of hatred toward the Hungarian minority.

Appendix C
Bossy's Report of August 19, 1938, to the Romanian Minister of Foreign Affairs on the Latest Negotiations with Kánya

. . . In view of the recent measures taken by us to protect the rights of minorities, on August 6, I asked the Hungarian Minister of Foreign Affairs to drop the intransigent position he has held until now and to accept, in the declaration called for in the Additional Protocol of our agreement, a formula that would not mention directly the issue of minorities.

Kánya did not conceal the satisfaction of the Hungarian government and public opinion at our gesture. This gesture, he stated, further strengthens his position toward Hungarian public opinion, and will probably allow him to accept our formula, with only minor and insignificant editorial changes. . . . But he added that he was not yet committing himself in this regard, wanting first to consult his department's jurists on the wording to be adopted, taking into account Czechoslovakia's special situation. . . .

On August 11 Mr. Renyey, Hungary's chargé d'affaires . . . delivered to Your Excellency a memorandum containing the Hungarian counterproposals.[1] These counterproposals resemble the ideas Mr. Kánya expressed to me, but in a significantly different form from what he had suggested. True, the deletion of the word "administrative" is demanded, but not in order to allow an identical wording for Czechoslovakia. That wording is meant only for the mutual declarations between Romania, Yugoslavia, and Hungary. In the case of Czechoslovakia, apart from the inclusion of the words "constitutional and legislative," a paragraph is

[1]See text in Appendix D.

proposed that would imply an additional international obligation. Moreover, as is clearly stated in the memorandum, the Hungarian government is not prepared to give the Czechoslovak government a declaration identical to the one received, but "Hungary would, of course, issue to Czechoslovakia the same declaration as the one agreed to for Romania and Yugoslavia, and that—apart from any other consideration—for the reason that Czechoslovakia's situation, from the viewpoint of European politics, differs considerably from that of Hungary or of Romania and Yugoslavia."

On August 12, I was called to the Ministry of Foreign Affairs where Baron Apor, secretary of state at the Ministry, handed me in Mr. Kánya's name a copy of the memorandum rejected the preceding day in Bucharest. . . . I immediately indicated to my interlocutor Romania's objections, and gave him at the same time the text we propose for the mutual declarations between Romania, Yugoslavia, and Hungary. . . as well as the text we propose for mutual declarations between Czechoslovakia and Hungary. I of course insisted on the imperative necessity of an absolute reciprocity—at least in form, if not in substance—of the declarations issued by Czechoslovakia and Hungary.

Mr. Kánya told me there was no reason for such an absolute reciprocity. Hungary was a unitary state with a Slovak minority—similar to Romania and Yugoslavia—while Czechoslovakia was a conglomerate of people. "The Slovaks are a minority in Hungary," he said, "while the Magyars are one of the constituent nationalities of the Czechoslovak state. The issue cannot therefore be dealt with identically. We are making no change in the present regime for minorities. It is up to the Czechs to henceforth draw up a statute of nationalities."

I replied that these were considerations regarding future procedures for putting into effect the principles of the declaration, a matter that was inappropriate for me to discuss now. But the principles embodied in the declaration had to be the same for all contracting states. "Even Great Britain," I made bold to say, "when it deals with the smallest of the world's countries, places itself on a footing of equality, while Hungary, which is no larger than Czechoslovakia, on the contrary insists on discrimination in its favor. This pretension is the more groundless since there is no reason to suppose that Czechoslovakia would demand identical procedures for *putting into effect* the declaration's principles. It only demands an identical *wording* of these principles."

Mr. Kánya remarked that, irrespective of the above reason, it was impossible for him to face the Hungarian public, whose eyes are now riveted on their kinsmen in Slovakia, with a treaty in which Czechoslovakia would promise Hungary only those provisions regarding minorities that the latter would in any case eventually receive.

As for the actual wording proposed for the exchange of declarations with Czechoslovakia, he considered it inadequate. He was satisfied, by contrast, with the texts of the declarations with Romania and Yugoslavia, and he assured me that the prime minister would also accept them.

I stressed the need for an official, clear, and prompt reply, since the whole matter had to be settled before the beginning of the Bled meeting.[2] Mr. Kánya asked me if this was an ultimatum, in which case he would not receive it. I replied that this was not an ultimatum, but that at Bled the progress of the negotiations would be reviewed and responsibilities assigned, in the sight of the entire international community.

Mr. Kánya asked me then whether we—the Romanians, the Yugoslavs, and the Hungarians—could initial the protocol and issue the communiqué appended to the memorandum of August 11, the actual signing taking place at a later date, along with the Czechoslovaks after they had resolved their nationalities' problem. Because I categorically refused to discuss any possible solution that would imply—even indirectly—a dissociation from Czechoslovakia, the foreign minister sounded me out on the possibility of issuing that same communiqué but replacing the names "Romania and Yugoslavia" by "the States of the Little Entente."

Without calling attention to the fact that this was the first time Hungary had proposed using the collective name *Little Entente,* I said I would be unable to transmit such a suggestion unless it followed from a gentlemen's agreement about all the clauses of the protocol. Mr. Kánya said he would ask me to call on him as soon as he had consulted the prime minister and two other government colleagues.

Mr. Kánya's startling suggestion amounted in fact to an acceptance, in the form of a *communiqué* rather than of a *protocol,* of the first proposal we made last year for a détente with Hungary—that is, a recognition of Hungary's parity of rights, against a mutual reconfirmation of the nonaggression commitments, with no mention of the minorities issue. The suggestion was, of course, the result of the written and oral démarches of Mr. Gascoigne, the British chargé d'affaires, which confirmed "the interest shown by Britain in a speedy and favorable conclusion of the negotiations now in progress."

---

[2]Meeting of the Little Entente, initially scheduled for August 20, but then postponed to the next day so as not to coincide with the Hungarian national day.

On August 18, Mr. Kánya summoned me to give his official answer, which did not differ much from what he had told me two days earlier:

1. The Hungarian government accepts without any modification our wording for the exchange of declarations between Romania, Yugoslavia, and Hungary.
2. The Hungarian government agrees to the elimination from Czechoslovakia's declaration of the word "constitutional," contenting itself with "legislative and administrative measures," but wants to replace the last part of our text by "in order to settle the issue of nationalities in Czechoslovakia, restoring calm and bringing about confidence within the Hungarian nationality."
3. The Hungarian government cannot proffer to the Czechoslovak government the same wording, but will make a statement identical to that given to the Romanian governments.

I told Hungary's minister of foreign affairs that:

1. I took cognizance with satisfaction of his acceptance of our wording for the exchange of statements between Romania, Yugoslavia, and Hungary.
2. I was receiving for information purposes only his new wording for Czechoslovakia's statement, but refused to take official cognizance of it so long as he did not accept the principle of reciprocity.
3. The rejection by the Hungarian government of the principle of reciprocity, in as far as the exchange of statements with Czechoslovakia is concerned, brought our discussions of the matter to an end—my instructions enjoining me to tell him that there is no longer time to make new proposals to Prague and Belgrade and that if he maintains his position, the entire issue will have to be reconsidered when the Little Entente meets in Bled, beginning on August 21.

I took this opportunity to explain to Mr. Kánya that the Romanian government had reached the limit of its concessions and that it had made the greatest of efforts to persuade the Czechoslovak government to accept, in the cause of our countries' reconciliation, a discrimination that represented a heavy sacrifice. I added that while I noted we and the Hungarians had reached an agreement on the texts that concerned us, I could not but express my regret that the Hungarian government has been unwilling or, as it contends, unable to conclude a definitive agreement with the Little Entente, an agreement that would have given an official confirmation to the de facto détente that now exists between us.

Mr. Kánya assured me that he, too, regretted that the current international situation had not allowed us to move further ahead, but both sides had at least shown good will. He understands that Romania and Yugoslavia cannot dissociate themselves from Czechoslovakia, and that Czechoslovakia could not accept texts that were not based on perfect reciprocity ("I knew from the start that it would find it impossible to assent," admitted Kánya). But he asked that, on our side, we recognize that the Hungarian government could not have signed with Czechoslovakia a diplomatic instrument that would have weakened the position of the Hungarian minority in Slovakia, particularly at the time of the Runciman mission. He declared to me that Hungary would not modify its attitude toward Romania and Yugoslavia and would be prepared, after the resolution of the Czechoslovak crisis, to conclude with the Prague government an agreement identical to the one with us.

As I cabled yesterday, Mr. Kánya then proposed—"so as not to burn the bridges, which would be in no one's interest"—that we conclude a gentlemen's agreement by which the governments in Bucharest, Belgrade, Prague, and Budapest agree they have reached understandings on a number of points (parity of rights, mutual reconfirmation of the commitments regarding minorities, the wording of the statement for Romania, Yugoslavia, and Hungary); upon agreement on the wording of the statement concerning the relations between Czechoslovakia and Hungary, the protocol will be ready to be signed. Mr. Kánya gave me a draft communiqué, saying he had made only minor editorial changes "so as to show myself even more conciliatory toward you," and he assured me he would also accept the designation "the States of the Little Entente: Romania, Czechoslovakia, and Yugoslavia." The communiqué would be issued in Bled or, on the same day, in the capitals of the Little Entente and in Budapest.

This communiqué, which appears to be a complete acceptance of our point of view . . . has of course as purpose to hasten the recognition of the parity of rights, which Hungary needs at a time it rearms at such a rapid pace. But as I mentioned earlier, one can also detect the influence of Great Britain, which seeks a détente in the Danube Basin. Hungary has always placed some of its hopes on London, as witnessed by its propaganda efforts in Britain; it could therefore not remain indifferent to a firm admonition from the Foreign Office.

I should add that the British chargé d'affaires was immediately informed of Mr. Kánya's communiqué, and he came to request that we study the issue with a receptive frame of mind, so as to avoid a stormy breakup of the negotiations. ("We hope you won't slam the door," he told me.). . .

Appendix D
Kánya's Counterproposal of August 11, 1938

The Hungarian government appreciates the Romanian gesture revealed by the promulgation of the statute of minorities, and it expects the implementation of the statute's provisions to be made in the same spirit as the one that inspired its elaboration.

In these conditions the Hungarian government is ready to accept, with slight modifications to the declaration on minorities, the texts that were delivered to Mr. Bárdossy on July 12.

Annex A. The texts containing the Hungarian government's final proposals are hereto appended.

The Hungarian government's acceptance of the texts in question is limited only to relations with Romania and Yugoslavia, the Hungarian government still being unable to reach an agreement with Czechoslovakia.

To bring the negotiations to a successful conclusion, it will be necessary, in the Hungarian government's view, to choose one of the following two alternatives:

1. Endeavor to obtain from the Czechoslovak government, with regard to the minorities issue, a broader declaration than the one envisioned in the relations with Romania and Yugoslavia.

2. Or conclude agreements with these two countries alone, and postpone their publication to a time when the situation in Czechoslovakia will have clarified sufficiently to make it possible to consider the conclusion of an agreement with that country as well.

With regard to the first of these alternatives, the Hungarian government would be grateful for the Romanian government to use its good offices with Mr. Krofta to secure from the Czechoslovak government the above-mentioned broader declaration.

Annex B. A draft of this declaration, which the Hungarian government is prepared to discuss as to form but without affecting its meaning, is also appended. Were Czechoslovakia to accept this text, the agreement with that country could be concluded without delay.

Of course, Hungary would issue to Czechoslovakia the same declaration as the one that will be agreed upon for Romania and Yugoslavia and this—apart from any other considerations—because Czechoslovakia's situation, from the point of view of European politics, differs considerably from that of Romania or Yugoslavia.

Protocol Draft (Annex A):

The royal Hungarian government, represented by ______ on the one hand, the government of ______ represented by ______ on the other,

Wishing to contribute to the keeping of peace in the Danube Basin and thus to create a trusting atmosphere conducive to the tightening of good neighborly relations between the states of that region,

Having undertaken talks on that subject,

Have agreed on the procedure to follow in order to realize the above-recalled [*sic*] objective, recording the agreement thus reached in the present Confidential Protocol.

I

The government of ______ shall declare, on its part, that it recognizes Hungary's equality of rights in the matter of armaments.

The tenor of this declaration shall be as follows:

"The government of ______, prompted by a sentiment of trust toward the royal Hungarian government and convinced that the latter is firmly and sincerely decided to maintain the pacific character of its foreign policy, declares on its part that it recognizes Hungary's equality of rights in the matter of armaments."

II

The royal government of Hungary declares its unfaltering will to forgo any recourse to force in its relations with ______. This declaration shall be followed by a similar declaration toward Hungary by the government of ______.

These declarations shall have the following tenor:

"The government of ______

Wishing to contribute to the keeping of peace in the Danube Basin and thus to create a trusting atmosphere conducive to the tightening of good neighborly relations between the states of that region,

Reaffirms its unfaltering will to forgo any recourse to force in its relations with ______."

III

The declarations provided for in Articles I and II shall be issued simultaneously in Budapest and in ______ on ______.

Signed in ______ on ______, 1938.

Draft of Additional Protocol

At the signing of the confidential Report of this date, the royal Hungarian government and the government of ______ have agreed to issue, each on its own and simultaneously with the declarations provided in said confidential Report, the following declaration:

"In its wish to improve and consolidate the relations of good neighborliness between Hungary and ______, the government of ______ studied the main elements likely to contribute to that end and decided on its own to take, in its full sovereignty, all necessary measures intended to eliminate the difficulties thwarting the development of friendly relations with ______.

Signed in ______ on ______, 1938."

Annex B. In its wish to improve and consolidate the good neighborly relations between Czechoslovakia and Hungary, the government of the Republic of Czechoslovakia studied the main elements likely to contribute to that end and decided on its own to take, in its full sovereignty, all constitutional, legislative, or administrative measures to assure to the Hungarian people in Czechoslovakia the conditions necessary for the preservation and development of its national life in the political, cultural, and economic areas.

Annex C. The negotiations under way since last year between Hungary and Romania (Yugoslavia), inspired by the common wish to clear the way of any elements that would hamper the development of good neighborly relations between these two countries, have made it possible to reach an agreement. This agreement includes Romania's (Yugoslavia's) recognition of Hungary's equality of rights in the matter of armaments and a mutual renunciation of any recourse to force in the relations between the countries in question.

During the pourparlers that preceded the reaching of this agreement, other issues exerting a predominant influence on the relations between the Danube states have likewise been the object of a careful and kindly disposed study. The related negotiations, however, could not be brought to a successful conclusion, and this for technical reasons independent of the negotiating parties.

It is to be hoped that once these difficulties have been overcome, the negotiations relating to these issues will be resumed.

DECLARATIONS OF THE GOVERNMENTS

Romanian proposal

"In its wish to improve and consolidate good neighborly relations between Romania and Hungary, the Romanian (Hungarian) government has examined *all the elements* likely to contribute to that end, and decided on its own to take, within its full sovereignty, *all necessary administrative measures* intended to eliminate *any difficulty* liable to hamper the development of friendly relations with Hungary (Romania)."

Hungarian proposal

"In its wish to improve and consolidate good neighborly relations between Hungary and Romania, the Hungarian (Romanian) government has examined *the main elements* likely to contribute to that end, and decided on its own to take, within its full sovereignty, *all necessary measures* intended to eliminate *the difficulties* liable to hamper the development of friendly relations with Romania (Hungary)."

Appendix E
Draft of a Romano-Yugoslavo-Hungarian Declaration

Proposed by Romania and Yugoslavia in September 1939

Firmly determined to maintain an attitude favorable to peace in the Danube Basin, to avoid any aggression or recourse to force, and to foster by a conciliatory and fair policy an atmosphere making it possible to improve and consolidate the good relations between the neighboring countries and the good will between the nationalities living within each country, the government of . . . [Romania, Yugoslavia, Hungary] will satisfy itself, in a spirit of equity, that the measures liable to ensure the development of friendly relations with . . . [Hungary, Romania, Yugoslavia] are being applied.

Index

Hoover Archival Documentaries

General editors:
Milorad M. Drachkovitch (1976–83)
Robert Hessen (1983–)

The documents reproduced in this series (unless otherwise indicated) are deposited in the archives of the Hoover Institution on War, Revolution and Peace at Stanford University. The purpose of their publication is to shed new light on some important events concerning the United States or the general history of the twentieth century.

Herbert Hoover and Poland: A Documentary History of a Friendship
Foreword by Sen. Mark O. Hatfield
George J. Lerski, compiler

Negotiating While Fighting: The Diary of Admiral C. Turner Joy at the Korean Armistice Conference, Foreword by Gen. Matthew B. Ridgway
Allan E. Goodman, editor

Patriot or Traitor: The Case of General Mihailovich
Foreword by Hon. Frank J. Lausche
David Martin, compiler

Behind Closed Doors: Secret Papers on the Failure of Romanian-Soviet Negotiations, 1931–1932
Walter M. Bacon, Jr., translator and compiler

The Diplomacy of Frustration: The Manchurian Crisis of 1931–1933 as Revealed in the Papers of Stanley K. Hornbeck
Justus D. Doenecke, compiler

War Through Children's Eyes: The Soviet Occupation of Poland and the Deportations, 1939–1941, Foreword by Bruno Bettelheim
Irena Grudzinska-Gross and Jan Tomasz Gross, editors and compilers

Berlin Alert: The Memoirs and Reports of Truman Smith
Foreword by Gen. A. C. Wedemeyer
Robert Hessen, editor

Lenin and the Twentieth Century: A Bertram D. Wolfe Retrospective
Foreword by Alain Besançon
Lennard Gerson, compiler

A Question of Trust: The Origins of U.S-Soviet Diplomatic Relations: The Memoirs of Loy W. Henderson
George W. Baer, editor

Wedemeyer on War and Peace, Foreword by John Keegan
Keith E. Eiler, editor

Last Chance in Manchuria: The Diary of Chang Kia-ngau
Donald G. Gillin and Ramon H. Myers, editors; Dolores Zen, translator

In Danger Undaunted: The Anti-Interventionist Movement of 1940–1941 as Revealed in the Papers of the America First Committee
Justus D. Doenecke, editor

Breaking with Communism: The Intellectual Odyssey of Bertram D. Wolfe
Robert Hessen, editor

Dear Comrades; Menshevik Reports on the Bolshevik Revolution and the Civil War
Vladimir N. Brovkin, editor and translator

How the Peace was Lost: The 1935 Memorandum "Developments Affecting American Policy in the Far East," prepared for the State Department by John Van Antwerp MacMurray
Arthur Waldron, editor

War, Revolution, and Peace in Russia: The Passages of Frank Golder, 1914–1927
Terence Emmons and Bertrand M. Patenaude, editors

Recollections of a Romanian Diplomat, 1918–1969: Diaries and Memoirs of Raoul V. Bossy
G. H. Bossy and M.-A. Bossy, editors and translators